PREDESTINATION:
The Biblical Truth Series

By Joseph Davidson

Published by SRM Media

DEDICATION

To the three angels God has blessed me with in my life:

Sonja, Rebekah, and Makenna.

It is only through you three that God has allowed me to understand just how much He loves those that are His.

JD

TABLE OF CONTENTS

PREFACE

The Biblical Truth Series is written as a short, concise study on selected Biblical topics. It is my intention that the works in this series use, as much as is possible, plain everyday language and speech. There are of course, numerous works that you can read that will delve into expanse theological thought, and debate, and also use language and terminology that most would find unreadable. However, *The Biblical Truth Series* are written not just for the 'religious folk', but also for the untold numbers that desire a deeper understanding of theological matters who do not consider themselves 'religious'. These are written in the spirit of how I view God's Word, that being that it was written for all mankind.

It is my hope, that through this series you might begin a lifelong journey through the Word of God that will greatly enrich your walk with Him. God's Word was never intended to be the exclusive property of any group of people. Furthermore, those of us who call ourselves Christian should desire nothing short of seeing all those who do not know the treasure of Scripture as we do, to come to a greater appreciation and understanding of its significance. As is the case with any work of man, it can never replace the Holy Scriptures; it is simply our testimony of its power and grace given us by our Creator.

May the works of *The Biblical Truth Series* simply be your springboard to a deeper study of the Bible. May they pique your interest in the topics discussed and allow you to grow closer to God. And, especially if you do not have a personal relationship with the Lord and Savior Jesus Christ, may they lead you to seek Holy Spirit that He might come to you and grant you the glorious introduction to the Savior as well. For this is the single greatest accomplishment that could ever come of these works. May they only glorify Jesus Christ to lead us all closer to Him.

The exaltation of The Savior of all mankind precludes all other motives for this work. I believe you, as the reader, deserve to know that about me. Yes, I have very strong feelings about the teaching of predestination as taught by those who call themselves Calvinist, but my motive is not to demean them in any way. However, if what someone teaches is an affront to the Savior, and His gospel, it must be corrected. Paul told Timothy as much in 2 Timothy 3.15-17:

> **And that from a child thou hast known the holy scriptures, which are able to make thee wise unto salvation through faith which is in Christ Jesus. All scripture is given by inspiration of God, and is profitable for doctrine, for reproof, for correction, for instruction in righteousness: That the man of God may be perfect, throughly furnished unto all good works. (KJV)**

Paul wrote these words to Timothy to encourage him to continue in what he had learned of the gospel, even though he would be surrounded, and even persecuted, by the ungodly. In these verses is the key to what this work is about.

I do not want you to believe anything you read in this work simply because I wrote it. Instead, my intent is for you to take what you learn here and compare it with what the Holy Scriptures teach, for they are the ultimate authority in matters of faith. It is my hope that those who teach the doctrine of predestination as believed by Calvinist might be made to know the error of that teaching from the Bible, not from me. If I believe that Jesus Christ is the Savior of all the world, and I do, then the first and foremost motive in anything I do must be to exalt Him.

J. Davidson

Matthew 6.33

INTRODUCTION

As I began to research what I thought would be interesting figures and statistics for this book, I was reminded of what brought me here in the first place. The issue of the predestination of mankind is a divisive topic! Yes, I thought it would be good to see just how the two different camps split up, and how they are dispersed within our different denominational groups. But alas, this seemed only to serve the enemy due to the enormous amount of disdain one can uncover when you began inquiring into whether a brother or a sister believes if they are predestined or not. The purpose of this work is not to stir up more discourse, but to admonish in Christian love what are fundamental errors of doctrine.

Hence, I will forgo any attempt to quantify the findings of this work with figures, quotes, or statistics, save for the Bible alone. For the sole purpose of this work is to discover and/or establish why we believe what we believe. Most of us are pretty sure about what we believe anyway, regardless of what we read or hear about the subject in question. It is only that sometimes, due to the environment that we have been raised in, we don't really know why we believe what we do, and that is a problem, especially for the Christian. How in the world could we ever defend something in which we do not know the answer to?

Neither, is this intended to be an attempt to refute the works and words of John Calvin, or anyone else who has ever taught of predestination. There can be no debate that Calvin was a very intelligent man, and one with passionate feelings about his convictions. However, I do believe his teachings are a product of the environment and time in which he lived. And as such, a person of our time cannot logically enter into debate with one who is dead and gone. If you feel this is an attack on Calvin, then it is simply because you are perpetuating what he once taught and have made it your own, basically you are a disciple of Calvin. Naturally, you might become defensive if someone questions his teachings, but I sincerely hope you understand I have no desire, nor inclination to engage in a personal attack on any person or group!

What I give you here is simply my presentation of the facts as I see them to you. How these facts are interpreted is up to you. This is the way it should be. Do not ever leave your view of God's Word up to anyone but yourself. There is no priest, preacher, minister, deacon, bishop, or any other office you want to name that should ever form your view of Scripture for you. Yes, you may find the words of these people useful in your search for truth, but ultimately it must be decided by you. This is one of the magnificent gifts secured for us by the death, burial, and resurrection of our Savior, the priesthood of the individual (Hebrews 10.19-22).

The truth of the matter is that there are too many scholarly works on this subject already. I do not haphazardly say that the study of God's Word is not profitable, instead, I am saying we need to rely more on our own study. Our culture has grown all to accustomed to hearing from the 'experts', without giving a second thought to what our own opinion on the matter may be. How much more should we be dedicated to discovering the truth for ourselves, than when it concerns the single most important document that has ever been, or ever will be...the Holy Bible. To even call it a 'document' is a monumental understatement.

However, this is the position most of us find ourselves in when considering the points of the Calvinist doctrines that are now under discussion. When we begin to discuss predestination, irresistible grace, and the like, often we find ourselves succumbing to the 'scholar speak' that usually accompanies any writings on such topics. Anyone who has ever tried to read John Calvin's work knows what I am talking about. Reading about the views that men purport on these matters leaves you feeling that you are simply unqualified to engage in such discussions. Thus, we are duped by Satan himself to leave these things to those whom we 'think' are more educated in theological issues than us. This is what I mean when I say that we need to rely more on our own study than that of others in matters of the Bible.

Tell me now; do you honestly think that God intended His Word to be so complicated that only a select few would be able to understand what it meant? Of course not, because He sent His Word to all mankind that the entire world might know His Son. The relegation of our understanding of God's Word to others is a trap of the evil one (Satan), for he wants nothing more than for you to feel inferior. Do not fall into this trap! You are just as capable of understanding what God's Word is saying as any PhD, scholar, or any other so called expert. The understanding is in allowing one's self to be led by Holy Spirit, which is something that all of us can do if we are willing. It was Holy Spirit who inspired the writers of the sixty-six books of the Bible to write what they did. Would it not then be logical that it would be Him (Holy Spirit) who would be best suited to guide us in our understanding of it?

Never forget that Satan's primary goal is to keep you separated from God. It is what he has been doing since the fall in the garden. Understanding his tactics will help you recognize when he is using them, such as using prideful men to sway otherwise trusting souls to erroneous doctrine. Thus, keeping you from a right relationship with your Creator and your God. This relationship is far too important for you to base it on the beliefs of anyone but yourself. In fact, it is the single most important decision you will ever make. The implications are eternal. Would you trust it to a man, or to Holy Spirit? God's plan of salvation is not complicated. In fact, it is far simpler that you might ever imagine! For in all matters concerning the Divine, God's Word is right, and whoever disagrees with it is wrong...simple.

Allow me to explain what I mean by this. The basis of what we will be discussing in this book is who can be saved, or to whom is salvation available, specifically. The Calvinist say that God alone determines who will be saved through predestination, or election of the saved from before the world even began. Then there are those, whom Calvinist call 'Armenians', that believe salvation is determined by the individual through their own choice (free will). It should be noted here that the classification of Armenian is not really correct as it ascribes a set of beliefs to a particular group, which in many instances do not necessarily hold to all those beliefs (i.e., not all those who believe in the individual choice also believe all that the original Armenians taught in their doctrines). This is similar in that what we call Calvinism is not really original to Calvin, for we know that Augustine was teaching it back in the late fourth and early fifth centuries. In truth, it probably predates him (Augustine) as well. These are simply classifications applied to a broad spectrum of those who may, or may not, believe all, or some, of the teachings of those groups.

Therefore, by Calvinism in this work, we mean those who teach the predestination of mankind by God before the world began. Specifically, that He (God) chose before anyone was ever created who would be saved, and who would be lost. Furthermore, the Calvinist says that this is in light of the fact that because God is omniscient (all-knowing) that He knew before time who would believe, and who would not (not disputed by this work). However, the crux of the Calvinist belief is the decree by God before time began of who is saved and who is lost (disputed by this work), and this is paramount to the understanding of this discussion. The terms Calvinism, Calvinist, Reformed Theology, reformer(s) are all used interchangeably in this work.

So, both camps (God predestines and God does not predestine) are telling you what they perceive to be the truth based on their interpretation of Scripture. As these two views are diametrically opposed to each other, it logically follows that both cannot be true. Yet, both purport to be taken from the infallible Word of God. This is a seemingly irreconcilable difference between two views. Yet, it is not irreconcilable at all, as I will present later, when understood within the context of the whole of Scripture. The truth, as always, is in God's Word.

Any (and that means from the beginning of time) error that has ever come from the interpretation of God's Word has been man's, and man's alone. God's Word has never, nor ever will, contradict itself. It is totally and exquisitely infallible. Men are fallible; God's Word is not! The Truth is within its covers, He has proclaimed His presence in John 14.6, "I am the Way, the Truth, and the Life, no one comes to the Father but through Me." (KJV) Men, like me, can tell you what we think, or what we have studied, but ultimately it must be you that decides if what we say passes the test of truth. One must never accept the writings or teachings of any person at face value. Instead, always compare what is written or taught with God's Word for His is the final say. There will be men who try to complicate the Scriptures, either for pride or financial gain, or usually both. However, the simplicity of the Bible will always allow you to expose them as the false teachers they are.

Now, please do not misconstrue my calling the understanding of God's Word 'simple'. This is not simple in the context of being inconsequential or unlearned. This is simple in the context of being easy to understand, sincere, humble, or lowly. Yes, God's Word is easy to understand. Of course, you must remember that the understanding of Scripture is predicated on it being approached for the purpose it (Scripture) was given. Namely, the Bible's chief and foremost purpose is for God to glorify His Son before all mankind through the plan of salvation. Christ himself said in Matthew 11.28-30, "Come to me, all that labor and are heavy laden, and I will give you rest. Take my yoke upon you, and learn of me; for I am *meek and lowly* (emphasis mine) in heart: and you will find rest unto your souls. For my yoke is easy, and my burden is light." (KJV) Simple.

And nowhere within its pages does the Bible ever teach that it is only for those who are educated, or who have a scholarly background. Nowhere does it proclaim to be the sole possession of the rich, the famous, the powerful, or of an elite class. It does not belong to the white, the black, the red, the yellow, or any other color in the spectrum. The Baptist, the Methodist, the Presbyterian, nor any other of the innumerable denominations can call it theirs. It is not even the exclusive property of the Jewish people whom are its primary authors. No one can claim exclusive ownership, or interpretational rights. God's Word belongs to all mankind.

It is not the exclusive property of those who teach predestination, nor is it of those who do not. None of us are its sole protectors, guarding it from the corruption of mankind...please! The Bible is very clear in this matter, God's Word shall accomplish its purpose, see Isaiah 55:11 (better yet, read all of chapter 55!):

So shall my word be that goeth forth out of my mouth: It shall not return unto me void, But it shall accomplish that which I please, And it shall prosper in the thing whereto I sent it. (KJV)

11

You see, the plain fact of the matter, and what has gotten lost in almost two thousand years of academic butchery, is that God has never needed us to be His translators, nor His exegetes. Academia uses syntax, case, context, and all these other grammatical tools of translation to pick and decipher what they feel is the true meaning of this or that verse, passage, or chapter. But, regardless of what they theorize about in the classroom, or dig up in the desert, God's Word will not change. The Bible points to Jesus, it tells us about Jesus, it lifts up Jesus, it is Jesus in written form. God's Word has always, and always will stand the test of time. It was His word before time began, what in the world do you possibly think that mankind can add to that...absolutely nothing!

This is the point I am trying to make, that regardless of how scholarly and educated you may be, you will never 'know' more about God's Word than that poor soul who can't even write their own name, but has believed and taken the Word into their heart through hearing it as truth. Of course I say poor sarcastically, because in reality, that 'poor' soul is likely closer to God than the scholar, who thinks they can reveal God through their academic endeavors, ever thought about being. Do you not think that God in His reconciliation effort to mankind would make sure that salvation was simple enough that not even man could botch it up?

The Calvinist should love this line of reasoning, for it points to the immutable fact that salvation is out of our control, and it is. All that is except for one inescapable act...faith. For, without faith we will never realize a relationship with our Savior. Without faith we would never accept the invitation of Holy Spirit to believe in Jesus as Savior. Without faith we cannot see that Jesus Christ is the lone theme of the Bible from Genesis to Revelation, and faith is the binding that holds the pages together. Faith is what sets you and I apart from any other created creature that has ever been made, including the angels. This is where Augustine, Calvin, and all those who followed after got it wrong. Hebrews 11:6 says,

But without faith it is impossible to please him: for he that cometh to God must believe that he is, and that he is a rewarder of them that diligently seek him. (KJV)

There is no faith in the Calvinist teaching of the predestination of mankind before the foundation of the world. How could there be? What is there to have faith in? If God decreed before any of us were ever even created which of us would be saved and which of us would be lost, then there is no place for faith. The matter would have been settled with God's decree, for Hebrews 11.3 says,

Through faith we understand that the worlds were framed by the word of God, so that things which are seen were not made of things which do appear. (KJV)

God's Word settles the matter. Everything that exists came into being by His Word. Would it not be logical to conclude that if He says someone is saved, or someone is lost, then that is the end of it? God could not have issued the decree of predestination the Calvinist teach, and also need to send Jesus to secure that salvation for those He pronounced as saved. This goes against the very nature of God, namely His nature of sovereignty, of mercy, of justice, and of love. God does not 'attempt' to do anything, nor does He need a backup plan. He is God, He speaks and it is done, period.

Now, I completely understand the line of reasoning that Reformed Theology uses when they invoke the sovereignty of God. Really, He is the Creator, and we are the created, so there is nothing at all that He has to explain, nor justify to us. He is completely at liberty to do as He pleases, for all that exists is His. And yet, what is lost in reformed doctrine is that God does not operate that way with regards to mankind because we are a uniquely special creation. We are created in His image. Case in point. Do you want to do good? Do you like to see justice prevail? Do you think people deserve second chances? Do you love your family? Do you want to see the poor of this world to be able to provide for their own? So, from where do you inherit these characteristics? From your parents, your grand parents, and from where did they inherit them?

I believe you understand the point. We, being created in God's image, are thus endowed with the same characteristics of God. The only difference being is that we love, but He is love. We seek after justice, and He is justice. We try to do right, while He is righteousness. We show mercy to others, but He is mercy. In all things we are created to exhibit His nature, the nature that He simply is, and cannot, nor will not change (Malachi 3.6). The point being, that while God is more than at liberty to do whatever He should choose to do, we understand by His nature that He is merciful and desires that we be rescued from our sinful condition (2 Peter 3.9).

However, this rescue is contingent upon the one thing in this universe that is unique to mankind, faith. The angels do not have faith. There are no animals that have faith (mankind is not an animal, regardless of what you have heard in the classroom, or seen on TV!). The rocks do not have faith. The oceans have no faith. The stars do not have faith. It is only that unique creation of God in men and women which are the one thing in this universe that share with Him the characteristics He alone possesses. Just as Hebrews 11.6 says above if we are to please God it will only be through our faith.

Calvinism is adamant that there is no way any human being could ever have it in their spirit to search after God, this is exemplified in the doctrine they call 'total depravity'. This (total depravity) means that mankind is dead in their sin and they hate God. They will not look for, nor seek after God, ever. They are lost, and will remain so until if, or when, God saves them by His choice and in His time. It sounds all good and holy and pious and everything, the only trouble is that it is completely false. Always remember, the truth is in the Word, God's Word, not man's! What does it say in the last part of Hebrews 11.6? In fact, what does the rest of the 11th chapter talk about...faith. Specifically, the 'actions' of those who 'believed' what God told them, and they 'chose' to do something about it.

The last part of that sixth verse talks about 'coming' and 'seeking', which are both verbs. Hence, they signify action on the part of their subject, which happens to be us...mankind. That's what the Word says, not me, the Word. "He that cometh...", and "...them that diligently seek him" are what is recorded in that verse concerning the pursuit of God by mankind. But yet, reformed theology through the doctrine of total depravity teaches that this is impossible, not unlikely, but impossible. So, I ask you now, "When God decrees this totally depraved lost sinner to be saved through absolutely no action or belief of their own...where is the faith?"

The plain fact of the matter is that throughout four of the five main points of Calvinism, faith is non-existent. Total depravity, unconditional election, limited atonement, and irresistible grace are all faithless doctrines. Faith, by its very nature requires that two or more parties be involved since one must put their trust in the other. However, all of the doctrines of Calvinism stated above are dependent upon only one person, that being God, as mankind is totally left out of the equation. Thus, as such, there is no faith in these, only mandates from God that mankind has no choice but to go along with. Therefore, since there is no faith involved, we must also logically conclude that the doctrines themselves are unbiblical, for the Bible plainly states that we cannot please God without faith.

THE LOVE OF GOD

A primary component in the error of the doctrine of predestination according to Calvinism is the inauspicious absence of love. Not just the love of mankind, but the love of God. This alone is a fatal flaw for the doctrine that should doom it in its tracks. I know that the Calvinist will claim that it is God's love that has caused Him to predestine us in the first place, but this argument flies in the face of logic and reason. This is the very same logic that God has ordained to order the universe (Ecclesiastes 3.11). He is a God of order, and does nothing haphazardly, or without purpose. Allow me to briefly explain.

In the Greek language that we get our New Testament from there are three different words used to describe love. The first is *'phileo'*, which denotes brotherly love. Just think Philadelphia, the city of 'brotherly love'! It describes the love that exists between friends. Then there is *'eros'*, which denotes the love between husband and wife. You may recognize the root from which we derive the English word 'erotic', which has been greatly misconstrued by our modern culture. Many understand this as the ultimate expression of love...but they are wrong, very wrong.

The third Greek word used for love is *'agape'*, which denotes the ultimate expression of love. Christ used this word when He said in John 15.13, "Greater love (agape) hath no man than this, that a man lay down his life for his friends." (KJV) Sacrifice, that act of forgoing your own interests for the benefit of others, is the ultimate expression of love. Keep this in mind as we talk about God and love in this chapter, because it is crucial to understanding God's purpose, His motive, and His plan for mankind!

This is exactly what I mean when I say that the Calvinist explanation of predestination flies in the face of logic. Their view of predestination is that before Jesus Christ ever created one iota of matter, that God predestined, or chose, who would be saved and who would not. Which logically concludes that God decided before we were created who would go to the eternal bliss of Heaven, and who would suffer the eternal torments of Hell. Now contrast this with 1 John 4.8, "He that loveth not knoweth not God; for God is love." (KJV) And yes, that last word love, is 'agape', the ultimate expression of love.

Now let us quickly go back in time to our beginning, in Genesis 1.27, "So God created man in his own image, in the image of God created he him; male and female created he them." (KJV) We are unique, we are unlike anything else created, and we are made in His image. This fact alone conveys just how special we are to our Creator, so special that He formed us in His image. John describes God as 'agape' love, not He loves us, He shows love, or He will love, but He 'is' love. If we believe the Word of God that He is love, then logic demands that we also recognize that Love (agape) 'is' God. And, as a special creation of His, how great is the love that He has for us. It is simply beyond our human minds to comprehend how much He loves us.

But, the Calvinist tells us that God, whom the Bible describes as being the ultimate expression of sacrificial love, is the same God who condemns us to Hell before we are even born. Logic, and more importantly, the Word of God tell us otherwise. While, the Biblical evidence against Calvinism is abundant, the most telling book in the Bible refuting it based on God's love is 1 John. So, it will be from its verses that we concentrate the rest of this chapter. Remembering that, as always, Scripture is a whole. That being, if the conclusion we draw from these verses do not agree with the whole of Scripture, then our conclusion is wrong.

Let us begin with the 9th verse of chapter 1 in 1 John:

1 John 1.9 If we confess our sins, he is faithful and just to forgive us our sins, and to cleanse us from all unrighteousness. (KJV)

John is writing this letter to a group of churches who are dealing with heretical teachers. These false teachers were bringing up issues that caused those in the churches to question their salvation, thus John is writing to reassure the true believers. His methods of reassurance are centered on the evidence within the believer manifested through God's love for us. His message is directed to these churches, but is also a general message to the Church as a whole. The purpose here is to define what John means by 'we' and 'our' in verse 9.

These are two seemingly insignificant words that would otherwise need no clarification about what they mean, but according to Calvinism they would have a very restricted meaning. The Calvinist would have to admit that 'we' and 'our' refer specifically to the predestined, the elect, to those chosen specifically by God. Yet, John in no way restricts this statement with any qualifiers that would indicate that it is exclusive to a certain class of people. John did not say "we that are predestined...", or "we that are of the elect...", no, John says 'we' meaning anyone who might believe in Jesus Christ. John's use of plain language here provides evidence that the simplicity of God's Word shines through where redemption is discussed.

I ask you to think about whom it is that wrote these words. This is John the beloved. This is the disciple who walked with Jesus, and who listened intently to his teachings for three and half years. This is the disciple who stood at the foot of the cross and held the mother of Jesus in his arms as she watched her son die. He is one of the disciples who was in the room when the Son of God appeared to them alive three days after His death. This is the disciple who was there when this same Jesus gave them the Great Commission to go into 'all' the world. If there were ever someone that would understand who Jesus died for, then it would be John.

In fact, if what the Calvinist teach were true, then John's words need not have even been written. What would it matter what someone taught about Jesus because God has already chosen who will be saved, and who will not. This is the conundrum that the Calvinist cannot escape, that being that every argument they give for ministry, preaching, missions, or any type of witnessing activity involves circular reasoning. In other words, according to Calvinism, God chose the elect because He looked down through time and saw who would believe, so the reason they preach, witness, and do missionary work is because God is sending them to those whom He knew would believe. Likewise, the reason they feel that it is still necessary to preach, witness, and do missionary work is so that they might reach those whom God has already chosen, or predestined. So the one is used to prove the other, and vice-versa. Circular reasoning.

Yet, notice when John penned this letter he did not qualify the forgiveness of sins with exclusivity. He used the terms 'we' and 'our', which would be applicable to anyone reading, or hearing this letter. John does not mention the fact that those who were doubting had been chosen, and therefore had no choice but to carry on. On the contrary, look at what he says 'we' must do for forgiveness of sin, "…confess our sins…". So I ask you, why would it be necessary for someone who is of the elect to confess their sin when they have already been chosen. The Calvinist says they must confess because they have been chosen, once again circular reasoning. Notice now that the Calvinist own argument destroys one of the foundational premises that they stand on, the sovereignty of God, and completely eviscerates Christianity by making null and void the person and work of Jesus Christ.

The Calvinist extols the sovereignty of God, and because of this they claim that grace is irresistible. Therefore, you have no choice but to be saved because God had decreed it from time immemorial. I have no problem with God's sovereignty, this is not the issue, God is God, and besides Him there is no other…none! But, if His grace is irresistible, and you cannot choose whether you accept it or not, and this was decreed from before the foundation of the world. Then why would it be necessary for Jesus Christ to come into this world in the flesh and suffer as He did? You see, God is sovereign, so much so that if He decrees something it is as good as done (Isaiah 55.11). So, if predestination according to Calvinism were true, then the person and work of the Lord and Savior Jesus Christ is of no effect, it happened for nothing. There is no amount of circular reasoning that can explain this fact away, it is an affront to everything the Word of God represents!

If the very foundational elements of our salvation were built on the tenets that the Calvinist teach, then don't you think that John might have thought it necessary to include that in His correspondence to the troubled churches. Wouldn't he have simply encouraged them by letting them know that their salvation was out of their hands anyway? Wouldn't he let them know that if they are in the elect then they couldn't resist salvation anyway, they would get it whether they wanted it or not! But he didn't, and there is a very significant reason he didn't.

John witnessed the person and work of the Son of God first hand. He knew that the person and work of Jesus Christ was the only way to salvation. He was the one who wrote the words that Christ himself had said, "I am the way, the truth, and the life, no man cometh unto the Father but by Me." (John 14.6, KJV) So when John thought to encourage those who were doubting, he did so by pointing them to Jesus Christ, and the fact that it was their belief in Him that would sustain them through any doubts they might have. Look at what he says in the first two verses of the second chapter:

1 John 2.1-2 My little children, these things write I unto you, that ye sin not. And if any man sin, we have an advocate with the Father, Jesus Christ the righteous: And he is the propitiation for our sins: and not for ours only, but also for the sins of the whole world. (KJV)

John says that Jesus Christ is our advocate, but why would one who had been chosen from the beginning of time need an advocate? The simplicity of God's Word is indeed magnificent! We need an advocate because of our sin. When Holy Spirit draws you to God your sin prevents you from approaching Him, yet you have an advocate who will mediate your case, Jesus Christ. That is what His life and work were all about, bridging the gap between us and God that our sin created. The Calvinist say that Christ died only for the elect, the chosen, and the predestined. However, it is clear from the verse above for whom Christ is an advocate, because it plainly says 'the whole world'.

John recognized the distinction between those who were believers, and those who were not by his use of the phrase "…not for ours only". He was telling the churches that Christ has paid the debt of those who had already believed, but had also paid it for the 'whole world', a fact that Calvinism denies. Yet, if Christ died for an exclusive group, why would John denote the fact that He died for the whole world? Once again, this is simple. You do not need to be a

Biblical scholar to understand this, and that is how God intended His Word to be, it is indeed for the whole world.

1 John 2.29 If ye know that he is righteous, ye know that every one that doeth righteousness is born of him. (KJV)

Simple words. Notice that to encourage these believers, John points them to something that is a conscience act on their part 'doing righteousness'. John does not say that this is what saves us, but instead that the act of doing righteousness is an outward expression of those who have been born into the righteousness of Jesus Christ. Thus, they could know by their own actions that they are believers through their deeds. This is a totally reprehensible thought to the Calvinist, for they believe that man is the most reprobate of creatures that has ever breathed a breath.

Remember who you are, you the individual reading these words. I don't care what color your skin is, where you were born, what language you speak, or even what you believe right now. You are created in the image of the most High God. You are a special creation with a special purpose and you matter to God. God loves you. Yes, I know we are sinners, all of us. But, it is incomprehensible to me that God created us in His image knowing that we were bound for a Hell that was not created for us. No, God loved us so much that He established the greatest rescue effort ever conceived, and all one need do to be rescued is to believe that He did it. This is what John said in chapter 3, verses 7-9:

1 John 3.7-9 Little children, let no man deceive you: he that doeth righteousness is righteous, even as he is righteous. He that committeth sin is of the devil; for the devil sinneth from the beginning. For this purpose the Son of God was manifested, that he might destroy the works of the devil. Whosoever is born of God doth not commit sin; for his seed remaineth in him: and he cannot sin, because he is born of God. (KJV)

Jesus Christ came to destroy the works of the devil, and one of his (the devil) primary works is to separate us from God's love. But, if the Calvinist teaching is true, that God's grace is irresistible, and this was decreed before time, then the works of the devil are already defeated by the decree of God. Yet, John claims that it was Jesus Christ who came to defeat the works of the devil. Both cannot be true, and the whole of Scripture mandates that it was Christ who is mediator between God and man (1 Timothy 2.5). It was Christ who created us (John 1.1-3), and He did so for the glory of the Father (Revelation 4.11).

What we must realize is that every action, word, and deed of God the Father begins and ends with Jesus Christ. Predestination is factual, it is taught in Scripture, but it begins and ends with Jesus Christ. The teaching of the Calvinist that God the Father extends predestination to mankind is in error, He extends it to Christ alone. This is the one thing that Augustine, Calvin, and all other Reformed teachers have missed on, and are still missing on. Mankind is predestined, elected, or chosen only in that we first come to Christ. It is Christ who has been predestined before the foundation of the world, not man. (1 Peter 1.18-21) Only through our 'belief' in the person and work of Jesus Christ can we claim this election. God the Father has not chosen us (mankind), He has chosen Christ!

1 John 3.19-21 And hereby we know that we are of the truth, and shall assure our hearts before him. For if our heart condemn us, God is greater than our heart, and knoweth all things. Beloved, if our heart condemn us not, then have we confidence toward God. (KJV)

John offers further encouragement to the believers. How can they know that they 'are of the truth'? Because they have been predestined? No. Because they have been elected? No. Because they were chosen before the foundation of the world? No again. But, because we are not condemned in our heart. In other words, Holy Spirit has no need to convict us of our sins because we have already believed, and for those who are condemned in their heart (the conviction of Holy Spirit of our sinfulness), then God is greater than that condemnation, or is able to save us despite of our sins. No qualifiers, no restrictions, no exclusivity.

1 John 3.23-24 And this is his commandment, That we should believe on the name of his Son Jesus Christ, and love one another, as he gave us commandment. And he that keepeth his commandments dwelleth in him, and he in him.

And hereby we know that he abideth in us, by the Spirit which he hath given us. (KJV)

There is a very important principle within this verse! Notice that this command is from the Father, for John addresses Jesus as '…his (the Father's) Son…' in reference to the commandment, and this portends to something we need to understand concerning our Heavenly Father. That being, the Father deals directly with the Son. This is covered in depth later, but understand this now, when God the Father deals with mankind it is done solely and expressly through His Son Jesus Christ. God the Father does not deal with mankind, or any person, on a one on one basis. Thus, the commandment John gives us from the Father deals specifically with belief and love…belief in Jesus Christ, and love for one another that is a product of our belief in Him.

This deals with the confusion being wrought by the false teachers in John's time, and provides further proof of the believer's salvation. John said those who 'keep' His commands 'dwell' in Him. Once again, these are specific life altering circumstances that John is addressing for these churches, and he makes no mention that these believers are secure because of their election, or because they have been chosen, or even because they are predestined. No, John says that they may know because they 'keep' and 'dwell', both verbs…words denoting action on the part of the believer. Why would John even mention this if he thought for one minute that the believer's salvation was completely out of their hands, it would be totally irrelevant, and insanely illogical?

Instead, John continues on and says that assurance of our salvation (…he abideth in us) is found in Holy Spirit that is our Comforter and Guide (John 14.16-17). In John chapters 14-16, Jesus spoke specifically to His disciples about the coming of Holy Spirit and His (Holy Spirit's) work (John 16.8-11), which expressly includes the convicting of the sinner of their sin. Yet, if the Calvinist teachings were true, what would be the purpose of Holy Spirit? Everything that Jesus said He (Holy Spirit) was coming to do would be rendered of none effect if a person had already been elected from the foundation of the world. Calvinism, in fact, renders both Jesus Christ and Holy

Spirit *persona non grata* in Christianity. Fortunately, God's Word reveals otherwise:

> **1 John 4.7-13 Beloved, let us love one another: for love is of God; and every one that loveth is born of God, and knoweth God. He that loveth not knoweth not God; for God is love. In this was manifested the love of God toward us, because that God sent his only begotten Son into the world, that we might live through him. Herein is love, not that we loved God, but that he loved us, and sent his Son to be the propitiation for our sins. Beloved, if God so loved us, we ought also to love one another. No man hath seen God at any time. If we love one another, God dwelleth in us, and his love is perfected in us. Hereby know we that we dwell in him, and he in us, because he hath given us of his Spirit. (KJV)**

One could easily write volumes on the preceding 6 verses, for they are quite simply indescribable. With our voice and human language, this is about as close as you are going to get to describing God, three words "…God is love." This is the 'agape' love that we talked about earlier too. The ultimate in love, a love totally devoid of any self-interest, instead totally devoted to the good of others. This is who our God is, as hard as it is to wrap the human mind around. It is not what He does, or what He feels, it is Him. Humans may experience 'phileo', or brotherly love, and 'eros', or romantic love, but they will never know the greatest love of all unless they know God. It is this love that frees us from the bondage of sin through Jesus Christ. It is this love that allows us to pray for those who persecute us, who hate us, and even those who might kill us.

Calvinist doctrine is so focused on the sovereignty of God that it has completely neglected the love of God. Yes, we are the ones who turned away from Him. Yes, we are the ones who listen to our flesh instead of our spirit. But, yes, He still loves us. He loves us so much that John says He sent His Son to be the propitiation (appeasement, or satisfaction) for our sins. Logic demands that if Jesus was sent to be the appeasement for our sin before the Father, then that would require action on our part to accept it, and John bares this out. Notice what he (John) says, "…that we might live through him (Jesus)."

But, if what the Calvinist say is true, then why would Jesus need to come at all? Why would we even need appeasement for sin if God had predestined our salvation? God would have in essence accomplished the work of Christ with His election of the saved before the world began. Remember the sovereignty of God? It is real, and if God so proclaims, then it is done. This is the error of Calvinism, God did not predestine us, instead He predestined Jesus Christ. One can only be predestined inasmuch as they are "…in the image of his (the Father's) Son." (Romans 8.29, KJV) But, contrary to what the Calvinist teach, this calling, election, or predestination is available to everyone. Remember the 'whole world' above, and also John 3.16 says 'whosoever', and these are only two among many other places in Scripture that indicate that salvation is for all who would believe in Jesus Christ.

Consider this very important fact that is known to all of mankind. Love cannot, under any circumstances, be forced to be reciprocated. Yes, someone may love you greatly, but that will never require that you love them back. We can only love unconditionally, for anything else is not love. And here John is telling us that God 'is' love, not that He feels love, but that He is the very epitome of love…God is Love, Love is God! If you are a believer in Jesus Christ you understand what I am talking about, because through Him we now know what love truly is. We understand the completely awesome selfless act of our Savior coming to this world to pay for the sin that was ours. We understand that without this ultimate expression of love made on our behalf we would never have known forgiveness, never have known peace, and never have known love, true love.

I really don't think there are too many Calvinist that would have a problem with this expression of Christ's love on our behalf, but it is just that they believe He only did this for certain people, namely those that were predestined. They also say that this grace is irresistible, therefore you will be saved whether you choose to or not, the choice has been made for you. So I ask you now, how can the Calvinist possibly reconcile this belief with the fact that God is Love? How is it even possible that our God who is the very embodiment of love is able to force you to accept it, and reciprocate that same love back to Him? This would require a redefining of love, as we understand it now.

However, I submit to you that this is impossible, even for God. Remember, Scripture tells us that God is love, thus this would require that God change who He is (Malachi 3.6, James 1.17, & Psalm 102.27), and this is impossible. Thus, the greatest act of love that has ever been, or ever will be known must by its very nature be a selfless act that is done with no requirement that it be reciprocated. Grace is not irresistible, it never has been, nor will it ever be. If it were it would not be grace, it would be a Heavenly mandate that certain ones within the human race had no choice but to comply with, and it would not be love.

I do not broach this subject flippantly, on the contrary, I have the utmost respect and admiration for the actions of my Savior on my behalf. But, Calvinist beliefs have robbed too many of the love of God that He desires for them to know. Think of those closest to you, spouse, children, parents, friends, or others whom you love unconditionally, and whose very existence makes your life so joyful. Think about how much you love those around you. Now understand, that you are a sinner separated from God by your sin, yet you know how to love (you are created in His image) those close to you. Think about how much greater is God's love, He is Love, and how for one minute do you think that He could force, or compel, those whom He loves the most (mankind) to love Him back. He understands love better than any of us ever will on this side of eternity, but yet the Calvinist definition of grace basically tells God whom He will and will not love.

God's love transcends anything we humans can comprehend in our flesh. Holy Spirit has introduced and drawn us to our Savior, allowing us to come as close as we can on this side to knowing its meaning. But, what on this earth will ever compare to the day when we behold Him as He is. There are no words, none. God did not make His Word a puzzle book that could only be deciphered by a few elitists, or make it so complicated that you would need a PhD to get saved. This is God's Word from Genesis to Revelation, and we do not get to pick and choose those verses or passages that fit our beliefs, or predispositions, and make doctrine out of them. God's Word stands completely and utterly on it own, it is Christ in written form, and it is given that it might draw all mankind to Him (Jesus Christ, John 12.31-32). It is given specifically to, and for you. You do not need me, or anyone else, to interpret it for you, or try to tell you what it says for you to do. That is Holy Spirit's job, not mine, not the preacher, not the priest, not any denomination, not anybody but Holy Spirit. Look what John says in the following verses:

1 John 4.14-16 And we have seen and do testify that the Father sent the Son to be the Saviour of the world. Whosoever shall confess that Jesus is the Son of God, God dwelleth in him, and he in God. And we have known and believed the love that God hath to us. God is love; and he that dwelleth in love dwelleth in God, and God in him. (KJV)

Once again, John was an eyewitness to the very events that he now testifies of, namely, that the Father sent the Son to be the Savior of the world. John knows full well the implications of every single word he now writes, of every thing he says, and of every deed he does. He has been charged by the risen Son of the Living God to go out into the world and testify of these things (Matthew 28.18-20), and he knows of what he speaks. But, even now as he encourages those amongst the churches he tells them plainly that the Savior has come to save the world.

John in no way throughout this discourse to the troubled churches gives any implication, or indication whatsoever that Christ has come to save only a select few. If there were a time for John to firm up the doctrine of the predestination of mankind, this would have been it. He would not, knowing the consequences as he did, have neglected to tell the churches that their salvation is secured by the predestination of the Father upon them before the beginning of time. He would not have continually made reference to the Savior coming for the sins of the 'world' had he believed that, as the Calvinist teach, He did not. No, John makes no reference of this because John knows that Christ did indeed come for the sins of the whole world, and not just for those who Calvinism says have been chosen before the world began. Look at what John says in the following verses:

1 John 4.17-19 Herein is our love made perfect, that we may have boldness in the day of judgment: because as he is, so are we in this world. There is no fear in love; but perfect love casteth out fear: because fear hath torment.

He that feareth is not made perfect in love. We love him, because he first loved us. (KJV)

How often do we humans strive for perfection in what we do, but continually fall short? Well, John tells us how to reach it in one area of our life, love. Perfect love, oh that a sinful, flawed, troubled human being might be able to have perfect love. The end of the eighteenth verse in the passage before says that if we dwell in love (agape), and therefore dwell in God, then God dwells in us. Even in our imperfect condition, through the leading and guidance of Holy Spirit we are able to find perfect love. This is the love that the Savior has shown for us in paying the price of our sin. This is the love that allows us the 'boldness' to approach the day of judgment 'knowing' that our sins have been covered by the perfect sacrificial (agape) love that Christ has shown to us by coming to this world in the very flesh He created. This is the same agape love that God has shown to the whole world when He allowed the Son to come to take our place. This is the same agape love that Holy Spirit has toward us when He seeks us out to convict us of our sin and point us to the only way of salvation, Jesus Christ.

The Calvinist teaching of predestination is wrought with fear, it is founded in fear, and it is perpetuated in fear. John plainly says, "There is no fear in love; but perfect love casteth out fear: because fear hath torment. He that feareth is not made perfect in love." The Calvinist can offer you nothing to assuage the fear of judgment, absolutely nothing. How can you know if you are one of the elect, for the choice was made before the world began? There is no list of names in Scripture stating whom God elected, or whom He did not. Have you ever met a Calvinist that was not one of the elect, no they all believe that they are the elect. Their only offer of assurance is based in hoping that they have indeed been chosen, but in the end they do not know.

However, John's words offer us the assurance that we can know we are God's. Love, agape love (remember "God is Love"), drives out all fear. Fear cannot stay where God is, and if He dwells in you there is no fear of judgment within you. Your hope is found in the fact that God's Son has covered you with His atonement, and you are now presentable to the Father. It is never in what we do, except that we must 'believe' that He has done this for us. We humans try our best to make salvation something that we can take part in, hoping that somehow our attempts at 'being good' will carry some weight when this life is over. Alas, they will all be in vain, for all we can ever do is 'believe'!

This is how it was designed before the foundation of the world. Not that God chose some, and left the others to their fate in Hell, but that He chose Christ before the foundation of the world, and that through Him (Christ) we are chosen. Jesus Christ is the only predestined, the only elect, the only chosen from before the world began. The foreknowledge of God is that He knows that if we 'choose' to believe in what Christ did for us, then we too shall be as if we are just as He (Christ) is. And because we are loved first by Him, I believe we are allowed the dignity (being made in His image) to choose whether we reciprocate that love. God is love!

1 John 5.1-3 Whosoever believeth that Jesus is the Christ is born of God: and every one that loveth him that begat loveth him also that is begotten of him. By this we know that we love the children of God, when we love God, and keep his commandments. For this is the love of God, that we keep his commandments: and his commandments are not grievous. (KJV)

Once again, John does not say the predestined, the elect, or the chosen are 'born of God'. No, he says, "Whosoever believeth that Jesus is the Christ is born of God." Whosoever, the same 'whosoever' we see in Joel 2.32, the same whosoever in Matthew 5.19, Matthew 7.24, Matthew 10.14, Matthew 10.32-33, Matthew 12.50, Matthew 16.25, Matthew 18.4, Mark 3.35, Mark 8.34-35, Luke 6.47, Luke 7.23, Luke 9.24, Luke 9.26, Luke 9.48, Luke 12.8, Luke 14.27, Luke 17.33, Luke 18.17, John 3.15-16, John 4.13-14, John 11.26, John 12.46, Acts 2.21, Acts 10.43, Acts 13.26, Romans 9.33, Romans 10.11, Romans 10.13, Galatians 5.4, James 2.10, 1 John 2.23, 1 John 3.6, 1 John 3.9-10, 1 John 4.15, 1 John 5.18, Revelation 20.15, and Revelation 22.17. And these are just a few of the many instances within Scripture. The point being, the whole of Scripture clearly, and I mean crystal clearly, teaches that salvation is intended for all of mankind, and not just a select few.

John again shows us how fear is defeated in the life of the Christian, by love. One of the amazing principles of Scripture is that we know we are His by the love we have for one another. When the love of Christ is within us, the fears of this flesh become incapable of abiding within us. Gone are the fears of guilt, shame, incompetence, and unworthiness. Gone is the hatred of those who would destroy us with their words or their actions. Gone is the fear of doubt that we will never be good enough to merit God's favor. Christ's love has replaced that fear with peace, sweet, wonderful, serene peace, and it is this peace that compels us to share what Christ has done in our life.

This is why His commandments are not 'grievous' anymore. It is no longer a task of a soul struggling to find acceptance, or worthiness. Instead, our soul is at peace with its Maker, and longs with joy and enthusiasm to worship Him by striving to be more like Him. This is what His commandments are intended for, to help us to be more like Him. They were never intended to tax us into submission, or to cause us grief. Our God takes great joy and pleasure in seeing His children become more like Him, just like any parent would. God wants you to succeed, not by the world's standards though, but by His. John explains:

1 John 5.4-5 For whatsoever is born of God overcometh the world: and this is the victory that overcometh the world, even our faith. Who is he that overcometh the world, but he that believeth that Jesus is the Son of God? (KJV)

Ours is a world wrought in sin. Not by God's choosing, but by ours. We created the biggest mess that any child ever could! However, God, in His loving kindness, did not leave us to our own devices to figure out how to clean it up. We never could, but He can, and He did, through His Son, and our Savior, Jesus Christ. Through Christ we have been given the chance to overcome this world of woe, and this chance is free for all who just believe in what their Father has given them. Notice what John says is the key to overcoming the world…"even our faith". Faith is absent in Calvinism, regardless of how they spin it, there is no faith in 'irresistible grace', none.

Yet, because our God is Love, He extends to 'whosoever' might accept the drawing of Holy Spirit to 'believe' in what Christ has accomplished through His life, death, and resurrection. This is the key to salvation in that it does not 'just' believe that Jesus was a good man, a prophet, or a supernatural being. Instead, we must believe that He is the Son of God. That belief encompasses the whole of Scripture that explains the person and work of Jesus Christ in coming for the sins of the 'whole world'. John says, "Who is he that overcometh…?", those who are predestined, no. Those who are of the elect, no. Those who have been chosen, no again. It is those who 'believe' that Jesus Christ is the Son of God, the One predestined, the One elect, and the One chosen from the foundation of the world. The one who 'believes' that Christ is who He said He was.

1 John 5.9-12 If we receive the witness of men, the witness of God is greater: for this is the witness of God which he hath testified of his Son. He that believeth on the Son of God hath the witness in himself: he that believeth not God hath made him a liar; because he believeth not the record that God gave of his Son. And this is the record, that God hath given to us eternal life, and this life is in his Son. He that hath the Son hath life; and he that hath not the Son of God hath not life. (KJV)

As John says then, so it is now. How often will we latch on to what some man says and accept it as truth, but spurn the Word of God as false. Yet, John tells us clearly what should be such a simple conclusion; God's Word is greater. Men can translate, interpret, exegete, and whatever else academia and scholars can think of, but they will never change the Word of the Living God. No matter the language, the text, or the time, God's Word remains the same. Consider this one often overlooked fact as evidence, the veil of the temple. Upon the death of Christ on the cross, right after His work was accomplished, that veil that was intended to keep everyone but the high priest out of the Holy of Holies, was torn in two…from top to bottom! (Matthew 27.51, Mark 15.38, and Luke 23.45)

Paul explains the significance of this in Hebrews 9.11-14, and 10.19-25, as we no longer have need of the high priest to enter into the Holy of Holies on our behalf. But Paul says that 'we' now have 'boldness' (see 1 John 4.17-19 above) by Jesus to enter therein ourselves. Paul is speaking spiritually of course, not that we are required to enter into a temple to make atonement for our sin, for that is what Christ accomplished with His sacrifice. Instead, Paul is speaking of our assurance in knowing that through Christ we are now empowered to approach God ourselves. You do not need the services of an earthly mediator (preacher, priest, or whatever), because you have a Heavenly Mediator, Jesus Christ!

Think about this, God has sent His Son so that we might have forgiveness of sin, all of us, and has made Him available to all who will heed Holy Spirit's call. Thus, why would He then give us a 'record', His Word, so complex, or incomprehensible that only a few could understand it. Calvinist, or anyone else for that matter, who would tell you that you are unable to truly understand God's Word are the ones who do not understand it. The work and task of revealing the Word of God to mankind belongs to Holy Spirit, and to Him alone. (John 16.7-14) Regardless of what anyone tells you, myself included, if it is not substantiated by the 'whole' of Scripture, then it is not His Word, it is theirs.

John says the one who believes on the Son of God has '...the witness in himself'. What a bold and audacious concept that the Creator (Jesus Christ) has a personal, one on one relationship with the created. Thus removing the middle man (the High Priest) from the God to man relationship. Christ has provided us this boldness, and desires for our relationship to God to be restored...through Him (Jesus). No man can claim to be your mediator, for that belongs to Jesus Christ and Him alone. (1 Timothy 2.5) This was one of the major accusations against the Roman Catholic church during the reformation, that the pope was known as the 'vicar' of Christ, literally, the 'substitute' of Christ on earth. Yet, Scripture clearly shows that there was not, are not, nor will there ever be a substitute for Christ.

1 John 5.13 These things have I written unto you that believe on the name of the Son of God; that ye may know that ye have eternal life, and that ye may believe on the name of the Son of God. (KJV)

All these words that John has written to these churches were for this purpose, namely the assurance of eternal life and belief in the Son of

God. And yet, not one time did John give any indication, offer any teaching, or even broach the subject that this assurance and belief is offered only to certain individuals. No, he continually reminded these believers that Christ had come for the 'whole world'. While Calvinism is a reach when supported by only parts of Scripture, it completely and utterly falls apart in the light of the overall whole of Scripture. Much like the Pharisees and Sadducees of Jesus' day, they have attempted to commandeer Scripture to suit their own interest, instead of allowing God to use it (Scripture) for His expressed purpose.

There are many opinions about the purpose of God's Word, and we men like to study it and ascribe 'purposes' and 'themes' for different passages or books within the Bible. But, its purpose and theme are succinctly summed up in one Word…Jesus. That is it. He is it. After Christ's resurrection, He appeared to two of the disciples on the road to Emmaus and gave one of the greatest Bible lessons ever. (Luke 24.13-49) In this lesson Jesus explained that all that had transpired concerning Himself was according to Scripture (Luke 24.27, 44-48), which for them was what we now call the Old Testament, or Moses, the prophets, and the psalms as they were often known to the Jewish people of that day.

Thus, the whole of Scripture is all about Jesus, and this has been God's intention from the foundations of the world, that His Son might be glorified before those whom He (Jesus) had created. (John 17.1-5) God's Word was not given to teach us moral lessons, or to speak against social injustice, or even as a guideline for the laws of any nation. It was given to lift up Jesus Christ to a lost humanity. (John 12.23-32) This is what John was telling us in verses 9-12 above when he says, "…this is the witness of God which he hath testified of his Son." This witness began in Genesis 1.1 and continues all the way through to Revelation 22.21. Every book, every chapter, every verse, every word, and every letter…it is all about Jesus Christ. The Word is Jesus, and Jesus is the Word. (John 1.1)

1 John 5.19-20 And we know that we are of God, and the whole world lieth in wickedness. And we know that the Son of God is come, and hath given us an understanding, that

we may know him that is true, and we are in him that is true, even in his Son Jesus Christ. This is the true God, and eternal life. (KJV)

Even if most of the world should proclaim that there is no truth in God's Word, we can have assurance that it is true '...in his Son Jesus Christ.' Any understanding concerning God's purpose, plan, and words are found through, and in His Son alone, and John offers this encouragement to the churches and all those who might read or hear this letter. Love is the only explanation for why He has given us His Son, nothing else makes sense in the light of who He is...God is Love! His love is not exclusive, for you and I know, even as flawed as we may be, that love does not behave that way. Paul said about love in 1 Corinthians 13.4-13:

Charity (love) suffereth long, and is kind; charity (love) envieth not; charity (love) vaunteth not itself, is not puffed up, Doth not behave itself unseemly, seeketh not her own, is not easily provoked, thinketh no evil; Rejoiceth not in iniquity, but rejoiceth in the truth; Beareth all things, believeth all things, hopeth all things, endureth all things. Charity (love) never faileth: but whether there be prophecies, they shall fail; whether there be tongues, they shall cease; whether there be knowledge, it shall vanish away. For we know in part, and we prophesy in part. But when that which is perfect is come, then that which is in part shall be done away. When I was a child, I spake as a child, I understood as a child, I thought as a child: but when I became a man, I put away childish things. For now we see through a glass, darkly; but then face to face: now I know in part; but then shall I know even as also I am known. And now abideth faith, hope, charity (love), these three; but the greatest of these is charity (love). (KJV)

Love never fails. The Calvinist think that if someone could resist the grace of God, and thereby choose of their own volition whether or not to be saved then that somehow impinges on the absolute sovereignty of the Almighty God, not so. In fact, His sovereignty compels Him to extend mercy to anyone who would accept it. He is our only hope of salvation, and He fulfilled that hope in the person and work of His Son, Jesus. His sovereignty is exemplified in His love. Being the very definition of love, God cannot be triumphed by anyone or anything, and is therefore sovereign. Yet, His Son set aside that sovereignty for a season so that He might come and dwell among His creation and redeem them from their fallen state, and it was His love that compelled Him to do so. But, now that sovereignty has been restored, and shall one day soon be manifested to all of creation. Salvation accomplished, sovereignty intact!

Could there be any other logical conclusion from a creature (us) made in the image of their Creator (Jesus Christ), than that our Creator will do everything He can to save us, even if from ourselves. Is this not what God has predestined in Christ Jesus, and what Holy Spirit is about the task of doing, revealing the Savior to a lost world? Look at Ephesians 1.1-14:

> **According as he hath chosen us <u>in him</u> before the foundation of the world, that we should be holy and without blame before him in love: Having predestinated us unto the adoption of children <u>by Jesus Christ</u> to himself, <u>according to the good pleasure of his will</u>, To the praise of the glory of his grace, wherein he hath made us accepted <u>in the beloved</u>. <u>In whom</u> we have redemption <u>through his blood</u>, the forgiveness of sins, <u>according to the riches of his grace</u>; Wherein he hath abounded toward us in all wisdom and prudence; Having made known unto us the mystery of his will, <u>according to his good pleasure</u> which he hath purposed in himself: That in the dispensation of the fulness of times he might gather together in one all things <u>in Christ</u>, both which are in heaven, and which are on earth; <u>even in him</u>: <u>In whom</u> also we have obtained an inheritance, being predestinated <u>according to the purpose</u> of him who worketh all things after the counsel of his own will: That we should be to the praise of his glory, <u>who first trusted in Christ</u>. <u>In whom ye also trusted, after that ye heard the word of truth, the gospel of your salvation: in whom also after that ye believed, ye were sealed with that holy Spirit of promise, Which is the earnest of our inheritance until the redemption of the purchased possession, unto the praise of his glory</u>. (KJV)**

The above passage is in Scripture in its entirety, but now go back and read the verses leaving out the underlined phrases. This is Calvinism. It removes Christ and Holy Spirit from redemption's plan. However, the underlined phrases above are the qualifiers of being chosen, holy, without blame, accepted, and predestined. These phrases speak directly to how these attributes are obtained (the Son), and whose plan it is to do so (the Father). Without these qualifiers it does sound like God chose certain ones before the foundation of the world, but that is irrelevant, because the qualifiers are there. And these qualifiers say that they are only obtained through Jesus Christ. We are not holy, He (Jesus) is. We are not without blame, He is. We are not accepted, He is. We are not chosen, He is. We are not predestined, He is. If we are to ever become any of these things it will be through Christ and Christ alone. When Holy Spirit does His work, and reveals to us the person and work of Jesus Christ, then we must choose.

In every single instance that you encounter election, being chosen, foreknowledge, or predestination in Scripture, you will always find a qualifier that points you back to Jesus Christ. Always! Yes, all the Scripture that a Calvinist will quote you is in the Scriptures, but it is always qualified somewhere in or around those passages as being expressly and exclusively through Jesus Christ. Moreover, so also is the Scriptures that tell us plainly that Jesus came to be the Savior of the world, the whole world. But, what Calvinism discounts is that the two can be reconciled logically, and not in some absurd fascinations that in no way fit with the whole of Scripture. In fact, they only need be reconciled on man's account anyway, for they never have been unreconciled. The Bible always has, always is, and always will be the completely infallible, and inerrant Word of God.

We were made to be in fellowship with our Creator, Jesus Christ, for the honor and glory of the Heavenly Father. This is why our spirit craves to know the truth about God, even in our sinful state, everything about us, within us, and around us points us to our Creator. We are unique in all of creation. In this vast universe, that only our God knows the limits of, we humans are the one thing in it created in His image. This is the beginning of the understanding that John is speaking of above, and it is found in the very One who has created us. Our sin changed the nature within us, in that we chose to seek after the pleasures of this flesh, instead of those of the spirit. However, it did not change our image, in His image we were created, and in His image we still are. This is why John says that we may know Him, and be in Him through Christ Jesus, "...the true God, and eternal life."

THE REAL PREDESTINATION

In the previous chapter we used the love of God to explain how the doctrine of predestination has been misconstrued by some well-meaning, and some not so well-meaning people throughout the Church's history. While most of the Scripture used previously was from a single book, 1 John, the bulk of this chapter's passages will be from various places throughout the New Testament. The reason for concentrating on the New Testament is the fact that most modern Calvinist teachings draw considerable doctrine from them, and as this is not meant as a scholarly work there is simply not enough time or room to touch on all of them.

Simply enough, the whole of Scripture can stand well enough on its own, regardless of what I write in this lifetime. One of the strengths of the Calvinist is their dogmatic adherence to select portions of Scripture that they use to support their doctrine. In this respect, they are much like the Jehovah's Witness and the Mormon where it concerns a narrow view of God's expansive Word. This includes using select passages to support a preconceived ideology (predestination in the case of the Calvinist), instead of allowing the whole of Scripture to convey its intended meaning.

As I noted in the introduction of this book, my research into this topic took me to many places where there was nothing but vitriol. You find the Calvinist saying those who don't believe as they do are unsaved, as well as those who are saying the Calvinist is unsaved. One says the other is ignorant and unlearned, and then the other says that they are arrogant and self-righteous. There is just way too much name calling going on in much of the dialogue between those who call themselves Christian. This is not to say that the dialogue is not important, because I believe it is very important. However, there will always be those who disagree with us regardless of right or wrong. Remember that Jesus himself told the disciples to expect nothing less, for the world hated Him first, so it would certainly hate them. (John 15.18)

The purpose here is not to belittle or demean a person, or a people, but to rationally and reasonably discuss what the whole of Scripture conveys to mankind. While the most ardent Calvinist will likely never listen to any criticism of their doctrines, there still may be some who are not yet so entrenched in its beliefs that they might discover for themselves Scriptures truth. Some might be in the process of searching for the truth, and hopefully will allow Scripture to dictate doctrine and not be swayed by the doctrines of man. This is not a contest to see who can get the most on their side, neither is it a I'm right, and you're wrong battle. Instead, it is a battle for the souls of mankind, and as Christian's we owe it those around us to be beyond reproach in our walk.

So, just as the chapter before demonstrated, ours should be a walk consumed by love. What does being a Christian mean, but to be Christ-like. Like Him in the love we show for others, even those who disagree with us. Like Him in the passion we have for those who are hurting, struggling, angry, dying, and lost. Like Him in taking His gospel to those the world might view as outcasts. Like Him in speaking the truth in love even when it might offend someone. He never tried to one-up anyone. He never had too. He spoke the truth...for goodness sake, He is the Truth, and the truth stands on its own. It doesn't need me or you to prop it up or defend it, instead our task is to simply pass it on.

Jesus preached every sermon, lived every example, spoke every truth! There was not, is not, nor ever will be any man, whether he be preacher, priest, scholar, or teacher, that can add anything to what Christ has done. Redemption's plan started and ended with Him, and Him alone. If any man tells you that he has a 'new' truth, he is a liar, and none of Christ. If any man tells you that you need his teaching, or his interpretation to understand Scripture, he is a liar, that is Holy Spirit's job. Satan has done a fantastic job in convincing mankind that salvation has to be complicated, and now we tell each other that there must be something more to it than just what Jesus did, but there isn't. We are just like the Pharisees that Jesus rebuked when He said, "You blind guides, which strain at a gnat, and swallow a camel." (Matthew 23.24, KJV) Ouch!

Christianity is not a country club for you to join, no, it is a full blown, all-out rescue mission to all of humanity drowning in the mire of its own sin. And the reason you are now privileged to participate is because you know the one who saved you, Jesus Christ. You don't save anyone, you tell them who saved you, and when Holy Spirit comes for them, they have a witness (yours) of His faithfulness. What an honor. What an awesome responsibility. This is why Scripture must be allowed to speak for itself; it knows just what to say. John 1.1 says of Jesus, "In the beginning was the Word, and the Word was with God, and the Word was God." (KJV) Jesus is the Word. The Holy Bible is the Word. The Holy Bible is Jesus in word form for all of mankind. You cannot differentiate. This should clarify for you the sanctity and magnitude of what is being discussed when you talk about Scripture. You are talking about Jesus Christ.

Now tell me, what human being is there from the past, present, or future that can counsel Jesus Christ. You know as well as I, none. Yet, every day there are preachers, priests, popes, scholars, professors, researchers, teachers, and self-proclaimed experts who will tell you that they can tell you what Scripture says. What they are saying is that they speak for Christ...I don't think so! Scripture itself tells us that God takes 'foolish' things of our world and 'confounds' the wise. (1 Corinthians 1.27-31, this is good!!) Do not be swayed by the experts, and the smooth talkers, for, as they say around our parts, they are "a dime a dozen". You want to talk about sovereignty. What about this, God takes our foolishness, and baffles all the so-called wisdom of men.

You must never forget that there has never been a creature more adept at self-promotion than a man (and I do mean this gender specific...sorry ladies). There is nothing a man likes to hear more than the sound of his own voice, nothing he likes to look at more than his own reflection, nothing he likes to talk about more than himself, nothing he likes to do more than what he wants. You get the idea. Man is a mess, all of us, no exceptions...save one. And it is that One that has earned the right to extend His mercy to whomever He will. That One is, of course, Jesus Christ. It was He who took on the flesh He created and lived a sinless life, thus fulfilling the Law of God in His flesh, and thereby winning the victory over death. God says in Ezekiel 18.20:

The soul that sinneth, it shall die. The son shall not bear the iniquity of the father, neither shall the father bear the iniquity of the son: the righteousness of the righteous shall be upon him, and the wickedness of the wicked shall be upon him. (KJV)

Jesus knew no sin. This is why death could not hold Him…it was contrary to God's Word. Yes, He is sovereign. So much so that death cannot hold what does not rightly belong to it, that One sinless life. This is why our faith must be in Him alone. There is no man that can even be mentioned in the same breath as the Savior, let alone counsel you on what God's purpose and plan for your life might be. His victory over death through His sinless life is what He now freely offers to all who would believe in Him. I ask you, what can man do for you compared with that…you know that answer too, nothing. We men are so prideful that we tell each other that we know what Christ's Church should look, be, or act like, and it doesn't even belong to us. It is His.

You want to talk about a real reformation, try this on for size, "And be not conformed to this world: but be ye transformed by the renewing of your mind, that ye may prove what is that good, and acceptable, and perfect, will of God." (Romans 12.2, KJV) This Scripture is talking to you, not some overeducated talking head that thinks that gives them the right to lord over your life, but you. All you need do is quit listening to the lies that the evil one is feeding you about your unworthiness, your guilt, and your incompetence. Those of us that have already had the privilege and honor of Holy Spirit introducing us to the Savior will be the first to tell you, that if you earnestly seek Him (Holy Spirit) He will find you and likewise, grant you that same introduction. He is faithful, not as a man counts faithfulness, but as the faithfulness of God. (Psalm 89.2)

I say all of this to offer you insight into why I write what I do about predestination as taught by Calvinism. It is not to 'prove' anything, as I do not have the authority, nor the intellect to do so. It is to tell you who saved me. There is no way that I would have been one of the elect, according to Calvinism. No, the only hope I had was God's love, the Savior's sacrifice, and Holy Spirit's pursuit. I was not chosen, I was not elected, I was not predestined, I was lost, but now

I'm found. Thanks be to God for His unexplainable mercies and grace through His Son, and communicated to me by Holy Spirit who convicted me of my sin. And this one thing I now know, that if He will save me, He will save anyone who will believe. For that is the only thing that I have done (believe on Jesus Christ), it was not because I was a good person, it was not in any degree I got, it was not in my life experiences that I learned it, it was not because I went to church, it was not because someone prayed on my behalf. It was not even what I prayed that saved me. It was that decision in my spirit, when shown by Holy Spirit that I was hopelessly and eternally lost in my sin, and revealed by Him that Jesus Christ was the only way I could ever be saved. At that point, when I 'chose' to believe, and confess Him (Jesus Christ) as the Savior, the Son of The Living God, it was at that point I was saved. Thank You Lord!

The mercies and grace of God are far beyond the mind of mortal man to comprehend, and yet He has made salvation available in the most simplest of acts, belief. Foolish right? That's what the world says, and unfortunately so does some of those who claim to raise the banner of Christ. The Calvinist is most certainly not alone in this camp, for history is replete with examples of those 'acting' on the behalf of Christ who were doing everything but that. All of these are examples of man's wisdom leading him astray because he is too prideful to let the Word speak for Himself. Pride prevents us from the simple act of belief. The same thing kept the children of Israel out of the Promised Land for forty years, as what will cause someone created in God's image to be cast into a devil's hell, unbelief. (Hebrews 3.16-19)

The Calvinist says that God chooses, or predestines, who will go to hell. On the contrary, the Bible says that if you go there it will be because you choose to, and not God choosing for you. (2 Peter 3.9) This is the inherent danger of the doctrine of predestination as taught by Calvinism, that you, or anyone hearing this heresy, might become convinced that the choice of your eternal destination is out of your hands, and thereby die in unbelief. This is one of the most reprehensible and offensive misrepresentations of the Savior that exist today. It so closely mimics true Christianity that it has come to be accepted as such, yet the two (Calvinism and Christianity) are entirely incompatible because they preach two different Jesus'. Paul warned the Corinthian church of this very possibility in 2 Corinthians 11.3-4:

> **But I fear, lest by any means, as the serpent beguiled Eve through his subtilty, so your minds should be corrupted from the simplicity that is in Christ. For if he that cometh preacheth another Jesus, whom we have not preached, or if ye receive another spirit, which ye have not received, or another gospel, which ye have not accepted, ye might well bear with him. (KJV)**

Yet, all around us, in churches, in seminaries, in conventions, in presbyteries, in bookstores we see and hear this doctrine perpetuated as if it were just another branch of Christ's true Church. As I write these words the very denomination I belong to, the Southern Baptist, has just issued a paper from its committee on Calvinism within the Southern Baptist Convention telling us we should all just get along because we are all really the same. However, Paul's warning above points to another conclusion, for he warns the Corinthian church about becoming "…corrupted from the simplicity that is in Christ."

The 'simplicity' of Christ speaks to this very danger that we see today. Men, complicating what Christ made simple (accessible for all), because of pride and thus throwing a myriad of stumbling blocks in front of those who might otherwise come to Christ. Like the false teachers that plagued Paul in his day, so too, today's church is also dealing with false teachers. These false teachers Paul said preach another Jesus. The True Jesus is the Word, and His Word reveals who He is. If one preaches a Jesus that differs from Him of the Word, then that preaching is false, and is none of the True Christ. Look at what the Word says about predestination and Jesus Christ:

> **Romans 8:29-30 For whom he did foreknow, he also did predestinate to be conformed to the image of his Son, that he might be the firstborn among many brethren. Moreover whom he did predestinate, them he also called: and whom he called, them he also justified: and whom he justified, them he also glorified. (KJV)**

If you are unfamiliar with Romans 8, then it would behoove you to read the entire chapter. For it is an extreme injustice to Scripture to try and make these two verses stand on their own. Even on their own merit, there is still no case for the predestination of mankind in these verses. Romans 8 begins with Jesus Christ in verse 1, and ends with Jesus Christ in verse 39, as well as in the 37 verses in between. The use of the conjunction 'For' to begin the sentence in verse 29 indicates that what is being said now in verses 29-30 is based upon a precursory statement in the verse before, verse 28, which says, "And we know that all things work together for good to them that love God, to them who are the called according to his purpose." (KJV)

This is another verse (verse 28) that is used out of context quite a bit, but that is another story. Look at what Paul ends that verse with, "…to them who are the called *according to his purpose*." (emphasis mine) So, this qualifying phrase 'according to his purpose' subjugates (brings under complete control) the "…all things work together…" statement before, and the "…whom he did foreknow…" one after it. Thus, the question might be asked, "What is God's purpose?" Oh, how many times has that question been asked! This also is another story, but there is one thing concerning His purpose that I can tell you of a certainty, I know where it originates, and with whom you can find your answers. Paul wrote another letter to a young preacher named Timothy, and in 2 Timothy 1.9 he said this:

Who hath saved us, and called us with an holy calling, not according to our works, but according to his own purpose and grace, which was given us in Christ Jesus before the world began, (KJV)

God's 'purpose' and 'grace' were entrusted to His Son, and our Savior, Jesus Christ before the world began. A gift so precious for mankind that only the One could be trusted with it, and God would be sure that it would reach its destination. An example, if there ever was one, that God deals with mankind exclusively through His Son. You want to find out God's purpose for you, it is with His Son, and with Him alone. Even better than that, look at what Paul says next in 2 Timothy 1.10:

But is now made manifest by the appearing of our Saviour Jesus Christ, who hath abolished death, and hath brought life and immortality to light through the gospel. (KJV)

What is made clear (manifest)? God's purpose and grace. How is it made clear? By "…the appearing of our Saviour Jesus Christ…", who has 'abolished death' and 'brought life and immortality'. And how did He do these things? "Through the gospel." The same gospel He lived for 33 years, the same gospel He taught intently to the disciples for 3 years, and the same gospel He told them to "…teach all nations…" unto in Matthew 28.19-20. This word 'gospel' is translated from the original Greek word '*euangelion*', and means 'good news'. But, it's not the 'news' that saves, instead, it's what the 'news' is about, hence, '…through the gospel (good news)'.

So those whom He 'foreknew' and 'did predestinate' (Romans 8.29) have been done so 'according to His purpose' (Romans 8.28). The same purpose that was made clear by the appearance of Jesus Christ on the scene of history some 2000 years ago. The purpose, that is the 'abolishment' of death, and the bringing of 'immortality' through the gospel of Jesus Christ. Thus, God 'determined beforehand' (the meaning of predestinate) that 'whosoever' would believe this gospel would be 'conformed to the image of His Son' (Romans 8.29). Foreknowledge and predestination are 'given us in Christ' (2 Timothy 1.9). God did not predestine any individual to be saved, He predestined Christ to be the Savior of all mankind! To as many who would believe the gospel of Jesus Christ (Romans 1.16). This is the real predestination.

Paul continues in verse 30, which begins, "Moreover, whom He did predestinate…", with 'moreover' being a conjunctive adverb relating what is now being said to the previous statement. Thus, we know that those to whom Paul is referring to with 'whom He did predestinate' relate directly to those being 'conformed to the image of His Son' (verse 29), and 'called according to His purpose' (verse 28). Therefore, those whom are 'called', 'justified', and 'glorified' are done so 'in Christ Jesus', or according to the gospel (2 Timothy 2.10). To say that we have been called, justified, and glorified through a personal, and individual predestination of the Father is to bypass the 'gospel' of His Son, which, as we have determined, is His express purpose (to glorify His Son through the gospel) for the existence we have been created into.

Think of it this way, if you had been individually predestined from before the world began by the decree of God the Father to be called, justified, and glorified, then where does the gospel come into play? It would be totally illogical for God to send forth His Son to accomplish something that had already been accomplished by His (the Father's) sovereign decree. It would make no sense to send Holy Spirit to convict those of sin who had already been called, justified, and glorified by God Himself. Only by taking these verses out of context could they be misinterpreted to give someone the indication that God individually predestines mankind. However, when kept within the context of the whole of Scripture, one can perfectly see that God is accomplishing all this through His Son Jesus, and not on an individual basis.

I mean, look at what Paul says just two verses later, still within the context of what he is talking about in verses 28-30, in verse 32, "He that spared not his own Son, but delivered him up for us all, how shall he not with him also freely give us all things?" (KJV) Notice that Paul is not saying God 'delivered him up for the predestined', not 'delivered up for the elect', not 'delivered up for the chosen', and not even 'delivered him up for those He foreknew'. No, Paul says plainly and intently that Christ was 'delivered up for us all'. Paul was well versed in the Judaic Law, Paul was a Roman and a Jewish citizen, and Paul had seen and spoken with Jesus face to face. If he had understood the gospel of Christ to be an exclusive message meant for only a select few, Paul would never have used a phrase like 'for us all'.

Paul knew exactly what he was saying, and he knew why he was saying it. He was the one that Jesus had called (all calling comes through Christ!) to take His gospel to the Gentiles. This was totally incomprehensible to the Jewish people of this time, and even the disciples struggled with this at first. Yet, Paul understood that Christ had come to be the Savior of the whole world, and not just to certain ones. These were the times that the mystery of the Church (Romans 16.25-27) was being revealed to mankind. Christ was breaking down barriers throughout the world through those who were preaching His gospel. And one of those barriers was that the God of Israel is the One True God, and He was not just the God of the Jews, but of the Gentiles (all other peoples) also. The Messiah (Jesus Christ) that

Israel had looked for had come, and revealed that He was not just the Deliverer of Israel, but of all nations, and all peoples.

Paul uses the terms 'chosen' and 'predestinated' in a letter he wrote to the church at Ephesus. Let us examine and see if the use of these terms in this text could be construed to speak of an individual choosing or predestining:

Ephesians 1.4-6 According as he hath chosen us in him before the foundation of the world, that we should be holy and without blame before him in love: Having predestinated us unto the adoption of children by Jesus Christ to himself, according to the good pleasure of his will, to the praise of the glory of his grace, wherein he hath made us accepted in the beloved. (KJV)

So, we see 'chosen us', and 'before the foundation of the world', indicating that what had been done was done before the beginning of time. But look at the qualifying phrase that is between these two phrases, 'in him', indicating once again that what has been done was done so 'in him', or in Jesus Christ. As is the case with every instance of predestination, election, choosing, or foreknowledge in Scripture, all things begin and end with Jesus Christ. Paul's theme in this letter is that all things are under Christ 'according to the good pleasure of His (God the Father's) will' (verse 5). It is impossible to separate these verses out to mean any type of individual or personal predestination on the part of mankind.

What Paul is saying here is quite simple, and it is that God determined (predestined) before anything was ever created that through His Son, Jesus Christ, those who believe would be adopted into His family. This is simple, for there is no strange doctrine, or complex symbolism here. God's intent for all of eternity is to glorify His Son, and during our brief stint in created time, we are given the opportunity to be 'adopted' into His eternal family, through that Son. We cannot, for one instant, take the focus of Scripture off of Jesus Christ, ever! Every letter within its covers is a gift from the Heavenly Father that points us straight to His Son.

Calvinism, and Reformed Theology, completely miss this altogether. Their theology dictates that God is consumed in the affairs of mankind, and He alone determines their outcomes, even unto salvation or damnation. So completely engrossed in the affairs of mankind that He would totally overlook the person's and work's of the Son and the Spirit. Nothing could be further from the truth.

God is consumed in the affairs of the Son, period. Any works, acts, or declarations of salvation and/or redemption to mankind belong solely, and exclusively to the Son. Any work of convicting of sin, declaring the Son, or inspiration of Scripture belongs to Holy Spirit exclusively. Yes, these things come from the Father, but they come directly and exclusively through the Son and the Spirit. The relationship of the Holy Trinity is something that we men think we have figured out, but have scarcely an inkling of what it truly entails. The details of three distinct individuals whose spirit and purpose are so perfectly aligned that they function as one simply escape the earthly mind.

It is only through Jesus Christ that any of us can accept by faith what our minds cannot fathom, and that is that the Father, Son, and Holy Spirit always operate in unison, as one. There are no hidden agendas, private vendettas, or ulterior motives within the Trinity. From the foundation of the world it was determined what each ones purpose was in the redemptive plan of mankind. That plan has never changed, it has never been modified or altered, and it has never been abandoned. It is just as it was from the beginning of time, and the only part mankind has ever had in it is that they have the choice to 'believe' it, or not. Look at what Paul says later in the 1st chapter:

Ephesians 1.11 In whom also we have obtained an inheritance, being predestinated according to the purpose of him who worketh all things after the counsel of his own will: (KJV)

You will notice that the above statement is incomplete. As is common with those who perpetuate misunderstandings within Scripture, you must keep the passage in its context. Notice the first two words of this verse, 'In whom...', which naturally indicate that the preceding verse carries a precursory statement to what is being said here. It is totally irresponsible to pluck verses about predestination, election, being chosen, or foreknowledge out of the Bible and try and establish 'Biblical' doctrine with them. It simply does not work that way, at least not and maintain Biblical integrity. Paul says before this in verse 10:

That in the dispensation of the fulness of times he might gather together in one all things in Christ, both which are in heaven, and which are on earth; even in him: (KJV)

So, 'In whom' we have an inheritance, and 'In whom' we are being predestinated is 'in him'. And, 'Him' is Christ Jesus of whom Paul is saying that God the Father is gathering together in one all things in Him. Therefore, those 'being predestinated' in verse 11 are done so 'according to the purpose of Him (God the Father) who works all things after the counsel of His (God the Father) own will'. And His will is that all things be under the authority of His Son, Jesus Christ. Once again, no one can say that God the Father has 'predestined' them to be saved, one can only say that they have believed in the 'Predestined One', and as such are as He (Jesus) is before His Father. Look at what Peter has to say about this:

1Peter 1:18-20 Forasmuch as ye know that ye were not redeemed with corruptible things, as silver and gold, from your vain conversation received by tradition from your fathers; But with the precious blood of Christ, as of a lamb without blemish and without spot: Who verily was foreordained before the foundation of the world, but was manifest in these last times for you. (KJV)

Peter was writing to the churches of Asia Minor (present day Turkey) to encourage them in the face of mounting persecution. In doing so, he reminded them of where their hope lay, and that was in Jesus Christ alone. Notice that he tells them that they have been 'redeemed', not by earthly means (silver and gold), but by heavenly means (the precious blood of Christ). Here again, is one of the original disciples, taught by Jesus Himself, conveying to the Church what he has been taught by Christ. He makes no mention that they are redeemed through predestination, election, or foreknowledge, but instead refers only to the sacrificial death of the Savior on their part. If Christ had indeed come to save only those chosen of His Father before time began, Peter would have been privy to that information, yet no mention is made of this.

Peter does make mention of something that was predestined (foreordained) though, and that was the source of mankind's redemption. This is something that Peter was well aware of, that Jesus Christ was the 'lamb' chosen by God before creation as the one and only, true and perfect sacrifice capable of saving a lost humanity. Logic dictates that if this Galilean fisherman (Peter) had become theologically versed enough to understand the predestination of Jesus Christ as the Savior of the world, then he would have most certainly also have understood the choosing of those who would be saved, and those who would be lost. Yet, not a word does he speak about that.

Would it not seem pertinent at this point of encouraging the very Church that Christ had come to establish to have informed them that they had indeed been chosen before the foundation of the world? Would not this disciple, being amongst the very inner circle of Christ's disciples, have thought it paramount at this point in the young Church's history to establish for those who would come after them that they too should understand that God had already chosen from among them who would be saved, and who would be damned? Is this not a doctrine (the predestination of mankind) that this disciple would have wanted to, nay, would have been compelled to make crystal clear in the face of impending persecution of the Church? Yet, he did not.

The plain, simple fact of the matter why he did not is because he too knew that this was not the case. He never made mention of the choosing of individuals for salvation and damnation because it was never taught to him by his Master, Jesus Christ. The disciples were an anomaly. They were the one group in all of recorded history that walked and talked with the Son of God in the flesh. They were the ones who saw Him die in the flesh. They were the ones who saw Him raised again to life in the flesh. They were the ones who saw Him ascend into Heaven in the flesh. They have a vantage point in history that is unmatched by anyone that has ever walked on this earth, and that fact alone is what gives such power to their testimony.

How could anyone who witnessed what they did ever be the same again. It is the reason they could go boldly to their deaths without hesitation. They knew in what it was they believed. They knew in

Whom it was they believed. They understood the importance of getting this message out to the world. Their lives were not, nor could they ever be, the same for they had walked with the very Son of God. This is why Jesus promised that Holy Spirit would come to them to bring into their remembrance all that He had taught them (John 14.26), so that the world would have a true record of what had been done by Him. And never once is it ever recorded by Holy Spirit's inspiration of these men that God had chosen individuals to salvation or damnation before the world even began.

Instead, it was revealed to them, as Peter states above, and as Paul states in Romans 8 and Ephesians 1, that God had chosen His Son, Jesus Christ, before the world began to be humanity's One instrument of redemption. God predetermined that through Jesus Christ, and Him alone, that the world would have access to salvation.

FOR THE WORLD

In this chapter we will show how Scripture consistently reveals that salvation was, and is, intended for all mankind. In reality, the Scriptures themselves testify to this fact by their very existence. Think about it, in a world that has historically gotten it wrong time and time again when it comes to matters of the Kingdom of God, the Bible is still the number 1 bestseller, hands down. No book has ever been printed more often than the Bible. There are more ancient manuscripts in existence concerning it than any other work of antiquity. It is in a word, unmatched.

Yet, at no point through the inspirational process did Holy Spirit ever command that the words being penned were for a select few. Never did God direct the process of its compilation so that only a few could read it, men have tried that, but never God. His Word was given to the world for a very specific purpose, and that purpose is Jesus Christ. If God, in His marvelous sovereignty, had meant for only the predestined to have access to His Word, then it would be so. If God, in His magnificent justice, had meant for only the predestined to hear the truth of His Word, then it would be so. But, He didn't, for in His wondrous mercy, He gave it to the world, the whole world.

Why is it so hard for us to comprehend that we do not dictate the terms of salvation to God? Why is it so hard for us to accept a love that is beyond anything that we have ever, or will ever know? Why is this Word that is so prevalent amongst the nations of this world so little understood? The reason for all these things is simple. It is our pride, the pride of mankind that blinds us. This same pride that the evil one used in the garden to separate us from God in the first place, is the same pride that he still uses to keep us from realizing His truth revealed to us in His Word.

The evil one tries to make you think that God is vindictive, judgmental, and a tyrant. He tries to make you believe that God is so disparaged with you that He disgustingly will just save some of those that He created. He tries to make you believe that God's Word is outdated, old-fashioned, and irrelevant to our modern times. He tries everything at his disposal to keep you separated from God's love, but like everything he tells you, it is a lie.

Our God did not put His Word within the reach of a world of people who could read it, yet had no hope of ever experiencing what it describes. God does not let the gospel of His Son fall upon ears that can never know its grace. God did not protect His Word from the corruption of mankind for all this time to have it fall into the hands of people who have no hope of seeing its Light. God did not make you in His image just to condemn you to hell, even though you hold the plan of salvation in your hand.

Even though I have compiled considerable Scripture references here for the purposes of showing you God's plan is for the entire world, it really only takes one. And more than likely, it is the one you already know, even if you have never read the Bible, even if you don't go to church, or even if you're not religious. You have seen the signs at the ballgames, you have seen the bumper stickers, you have seen the quotes of that one indomitable verse:

John 3.16 For God so loved the world, that he gave his only begotten Son, that whosoever believeth in him should not perish, but have everlasting life. (KJV)

I have never understood how someone who calls their self a Calvinist can read this verse and remain so. I mean, how much simpler can it be? This is not an apostle or a prophet talking here, it is Jesus Christ himself. This verse is the prime example of the whole of Scripture's teaching that Christ came to be the Savior of the world, and not just a select few. There are no hidden meanings here. There are no complex Greek words that were unable to be translated that caused us to only guess at its translation.

This was Jesus explaining to Nicodemus how to be saved. In fact, not only does Jesus use the term 'whosoever' in this verse, but also in the preceding one as well, "That whosoever believeth in him should not perish, but have eternal life." (John 3.15, KJV) Thus, we know that Jesus was telling Nicodemus exactly whom it was He came to save, that being 'whosoever believes'. Nicodemus was a

Pharisee, the Jewish sect that believed in the resurrection, and a 'ruler of the Jews', as noted in John 3.1 at the beginning of the chapter. Would it not have been logical for Jesus to reveal to Nicodemus that He (Jesus) had come to save only the predestined, or chosen ones, if in fact this were the case? Why would Jesus proclaim to a Jewish ruler, who was looking for the coming Messiah, that He had come to save 'whosoever believes', if in fact, He came only for those predestined, chosen specifically by God before the foundation of the world?

The reason He proclaimed that He came to save 'whosoever believes' is because that is exactly what He came to do. To say that He came only to save the chosen few is a blatant misrepresentation of the message of the gospel of Jesus Christ, and the Word. Not once in any statement, word, or deed did Christ ever give the disciples reason to think that He had come to provide redemption to only those whom His Father had chosen before time began. As is the case with Nicodemus, every instance of Jesus proclaiming the gospel is done so with the intent that anyone who would hear and believe might be saved. Twice Jesus told Nicodemus that 'whosoever' would believe might be saved. This is not the statement of one who is come to save just a few.

Look at what Jesus said about Himself in verse 14, "And as Moses lifted up the serpent in the wilderness, even so must the Son of man be lifted up." (KJV) This incidence of the brazen serpent made by Moses is found in Numbers 21.4-9, and is one in which the children of Israel began to speak against God and Moses. Their bitter words came forth from their lack of faith, or disbelief, in what God had told Moses He would do. Thus, as a result of their unbelief, a host of venomous snakes came into the camp and began to bite the people, with many of them dying. Seeing the error of their way, the camp called on Moses to pray for them that they might be delivered from their affliction. Moses did this, and was instructed by God to fashion a serpent of brass and place it on a pole in the midst of the camp.

The brass serpent is what is known as a 'type' of Christ, which is an occurrence or an event in the Old Testament that points to Jesus. He (Jesus) acknowledges as much when He says to Nicodemus that He too must be lifted up as the serpent was by Moses. Notice God's simple, and straightforward instructions to Moses concerning the serpent in Numbers 21.8, "And the LORD said unto Moses, Make thee a fiery serpent, and set it upon a pole: and it shall come to pass, that every one that is bitten, when he looketh upon it, shall live." (KJV) So, a people who no longer believed in what God was telling them were saved by what, belief.

God's instructions were simple and plain. There were no elaborate rituals or complex remedies that needed to be observed or made. The reason for the people's affliction was unbelief; the source of the people's deliverance was belief. Those that had been bitten had only to look upon the serpent of brass to be healed, but what would cause them to do so? Moses had explained to the camp that God's instruction for their deliverance was to look upon this brass serpent up on a pole, and only those who believed what Moses was telling them would look upon it believing they would be healed. The message was given to the whole camp, yet you had to believe the message to be delivered.

This example of Christ reveals what part of redemptions plan was His to fulfill. He told Nicodemus that He too must be lifted up, thus speaking of His death on the cross. However, as Moses' message was for the camp of Israel, Christ's message was, as He said, for the whole world. This is what He meant by 'whosoever believes', it was not just that someone believed that Jesus was a real person, or a great historical figure, no this belief must be based in what He achieved by His death on the cross. His death on the cross paid for the sins of all mankind for all of time. From the first sin of Adam to the time when the angel shall declare that time shall be no more, the death of our Savior paid a debt that none of us could ever even think of paying. He became your perfect sacrifice before His Father in Heaven, thus securing your redemption, your salvation. This is what you must 'believe', that His death was for you and that only by believing in this can you ever be saved.

This is the message of the gospel, this is what He was telling Nicodemus, that 'whosoever believes' that Christ has done this for them will be saved. The Calvinist teach that Christ's death was only for the predestined chosen by God, but yet Christ Himself says that 'whosoever believes' can be saved. This is why each doctrine you hear from man must be measured against the 'whole' of Scripture. The Bible does not ever contradict itself, ever! You cannot have a doctrine taught in one part of Scripture that contradicts another doctrine taught in another part of Scripture. This is a result of the error of a man, it is man who misunderstands and misconstrues Scripture. This is what has happened with the Calvinist interpretation of predestination, they have misunderstood it because Scripture is plain that Christ came to 'whosoever'.

The Calvinist cannot reconcile the fact that they think the Bible teaches the predestination of man, and that Christ came to save the world. Thus, they say that Christ's death must have only been for the predestined, which is in direct contradiction to God's Holy Word. Yet, the teaching of predestination is no contradiction at all when one understands it as the Bible teaches it, that being that it is Christ, and Christ alone who is predestined. He is the Lamb chosen before the foundation of the world (Revelation 13.8), and it is only in and through Him that one can be partaker of this predestined state. God has never extended predestination to any man, only to His Son. You want to be predestined, then you have to believe in what Christ has done for you by His death on the cross.

It is through the substitutionary sacrifice of Jesus Christ that His attributes are given to those who believe in Him. Attributes such as sonship (through adoption), inheritance, and yes, predestination are attributed to us upon our belief in Jesus Christ. Upon our belief in Him (Jesus), the sacrifice that He gave covers our unrighteous condition. It is no longer visible to the Father, for He now sees only the perfection of the Son upon our life. So, everything that the Son is to the Father is what He now sees in us, including being chosen before the foundation of the world. Thus, we become as if we were predestined from before time began, we are completely and utterly saved from all our sin. Yet, it was not us that was chosen, but the Son, The Son who now covers us in the sight of the Father. Our advocate, our mediator, our sacrifice, our Savior, it all is solely and exclusively by and through Jesus Christ. It was never us that were chosen, it has always been Jesus.

So, it was never God choosing any man before the foundation of the world, nor did He predestine certain individuals to heaven and others to hell. From the foundations of the world God has always chosen only His Son. It could not be otherwise for the righteousness of God precludes such an act as choosing some for salvation and others for condemnation. Look at some of the attributes of our great God;

Psalm 9.8 And he shall judge the world in righteousness, he shall minister judgment to the people in uprightness. (KJV)

How shall He judge the world? In righteousness. How shall he minister judgment to the people? In uprightness. In his praise of God, David extols the virtues that belong exclusively to God. He alone is righteous, and upright. There is no man ever born that can claim the same, save one...Jesus Christ, His Son. Yet, the Calvinist declares that our Righteous and Upright God will proclaim before anyone is ever created which of them will be saved and which of them will be condemned. They claim that His sovereign omniscience allows Him to know who will believe and who will not, which is a claim I do not dispute. However, if He (God) makes this decree, it is done. He is sovereign. So now what you have is that multitudes of people have been condemned to hell by His decree, and not because of what they chose. They have no chance to repent (to change their mind, or direction) because the sovereign God had declared them destitute, irreparably lost, and bound for hell.

Still, the Calvinist says that because God knew this beforehand, he declared it as such. But, their tendency to exploit His sovereignty in these discussions belie their very argument. For our Righteous God would never condemn anyone without the possibility of repentance, which is exactly what the Calvinist teaching precludes. In fact, Peter, one of the Savior's most trusted disciples, wrote these words:

2 Peter 3.9 The Lord is not slack concerning his promise, as some men count slackness; but is longsuffering to us-ward, not willing that any should perish, but that all should come to repentance. (KJV)

Peter wrote these words while speaking of the coming judgment upon mankind, yet in them he proclaims what the Savior taught him. Peter knew when he wrote these words that Jesus Christ had come for the salvation of all mankind. Yes, there were, and will always be those who scoff at the offer, he mentions as much in this chapter. However, in His righteousness, God extends the offer for repentance to 'all' through His Son. If He had in fact, declared from the beginning of the world who was saved and who was lost, then why would He be 'longsuffering' because by His very decree, mercy would be irrelevant. The simple truth is that God has never made any such decree (who are the saved and the lost), because He is Righteous and Upright, and as such He is patient (longsuffering) that all will choose to repent.

Peter and John knew Jesus as well, or better, than anyone on this earth. Paul had a face-to-face meeting with the Savior. It is totally irresponsible on the part of anyone to think that men like Peter, John, or Paul would use words like 'all', 'whosoever', and 'world' when speaking of the blessed gospel of Jesus Christ and not have any idea of their ramifications. These men knew exactly what they were saying, and they knew exactly what it meant. They were teaching as they had been taught, that this gospel is for all the world. This teaching is replete throughout the Scriptures. Although these Old Testament selections do not deal with predestination specifically, they do testify to us of God's oversight and care for all the inhabitants of the world:

Psalm 24.1 The earth is the LORD'S, and the fulness thereof; the world, and they that dwell therein. (KJV)

Psalm 33.8 Let all the earth fear the LORD: let all the inhabitants of the world stand in awe of him. (KJV)

Psalm 89.11 The heavens are thine, the earth also is thine: as for the world and the fulness thereof, thou hast founded them. (KJV)

Psalm 90.2 Before the mountains were brought forth, or ever thou hadst formed the earth and the world, even from everlasting to everlasting, thou art God. (KJV)

Psalm 98.9 Before the LORD; for he cometh to judge the earth: with righteousness shall he judge the world, and the people with equity. (KJV)

Isaiah 18.3 All ye inhabitants of the world, and dwellers on the earth, see ye, when he lifteth up an ensign on the

mountains; and when he bloweth a trumpet, hear ye. (KJV)

Isaiah 26.9 With my soul have I desired thee in the night; yea, with my spirit within me will I seek thee early: for when thy judgments are in the earth, the inhabitants of the world will learn righteousness. (KJV)

Isaiah 27.6 He shall cause them that come of Jacob to take root: Israel shall blossom and bud, and fill the face of the world with fruit. (KJV)

Isaiah 34.1 Come near, ye nations, to hear; and hearken, ye people: let the earth hear, and all that is therein; the world, and all things that come forth of it. (KJV)

Isaiah 62.11 Behold, the LORD hath proclaimed unto the end of the world, Say ye to the daughter of Zion, Behold, thy salvation cometh; behold, his reward is with him, and his work before him. (KJV)

Isaiah 64.4 For since the beginning of the world men have not heard, nor perceived by the ear, neither hath the eye seen, O God, beside thee, what he hath prepared for him that waiteth for him. (KJV)

Nahum 1.5 The mountains quake at him, and the hills melt, and the earth is burned at his presence, yea, the world, and all that dwell therein. (KJV)

These passages all give testament to God's scope of service, if you will, which is consistently revealed in Scripture as the 'world'. Yes, we are made in His image, which alone separates us from anything else ever created. But, what made us alive was the 'breath' of God (Genesis 2.7) that He enlivened us with. It is Him that makes us live. We are each a part of God, and not in the pantheistic sense that the entire universe is God, and we are all a part of God. That is nonsense. What I speak of is an individual and personal connection with our Creator. The rocks are not part of God. The oceans are not part of God. The stars are not part of God. The universe is not part of God. However, you are. And, as such, He will not leave you without recourse to accept Him for who He is. Your Creator and your God.

The plan of redemption established from the foundation of the world was done so especially for you, and don't you dare let anyone tell you any different. God has not abandoned you, neither has He declared you lost. He has not left you, nor has He forgotten you. He is right where He has always been, waiting for you to heed Holy Spirit's call to repent of the path of destruction that you are on. God does not take pleasure in the destruction of the wicked (Ezekiel 33.11), but desires for them to turn from their evil ways. If there were any doubt that God's will is for the entire world to be saved, then the earthly ministry of Jesus should have ended that for there are numerous references by the Savior that this is exactly why He came:

Matthew 5.14 Ye are the light of the world. A city that is set on an hill cannot be hid. (KJV)

This is a statement from Jesus during the midst of the Sermon on the Mount. In this statement Jesus proclaims that those who choose to believe in Him will be the light of the world. But, notice to whom He is speaking with, for in the previous chapter (Matthew 4.25) it tells where the multitudes that were gathered on the mount had came from, "And there followed him great multitudes of people from Galilee, and from Decapolis, and from Jerusalem, and from Judaea, and from beyond Jordan." (KJV) Notice that Jesus did not instruct the disciples He had already called to go out and invite certain people to the mount. The people that came did so of their own accord, they wanted to be there and hear what Jesus had to say.

These people had come from all over the area because they had heard the reports of the ministry of Jesus that were being told. The Scriptures tell us in verse 23 that Christ was preaching the gospel, healing the sick, and curing disease around the area of Galilee, and people were starting to talk! There can be no doubt that Jesus knew exactly what He was doing and what the result would be. Why would the Savior do such things if He had known that only certain of these people were amongst the chosen? Don't tell me that the purpose of these things were just to reach those who had been chosen, that is an insult to the power of the gospel of Jesus Christ.

Jesus wanted as many as He could get on that mount. He wanted them to hear of the love that God had for them, and how He desired for them to live as He intended for us to live. He wanted as many as could be to be saved. If God had decreed before time who would be saved, then there would have been those in the crowd that day that would have no opportunity to believe. God's decree would have settled the matter before they were ever born. How can the Calvinist consider this the actions of a Righteous God? How can they believe that one as upright and just as the God of Israel would ever send a Savior to a people whom He had already declared lost? How? Because they do not understand whom our God is. Our God is Love!

Consider the teachings of the Savior concerning the end of the world when asked by His disciples how they would know it was near:

Matthew 24.14 And this gospel of the kingdom shall be preached in all the world for a witness unto all nations; and then shall the end come. (KJV)

This verse perfectly exemplifies the righteousness and uprightness of God that David proclaimed in the Psalm we looked at earlier. Jesus declares to His disciples that before this world shall end that His gospel shall be preached 'in all the world', and it is so that it might be 'a witness' to 'all nations'. The Greek word for witness in that verse is '*martyrion*', which simply means testimony. In other words, it is Christ's intention that all hear the gospel. The reason being is that no one can be guilty of unbelief if they haven't been told what to believe, hence the witness, or testimony, to all nations.

This is the same concept that we see today in any court of law, that being that the quickest way to prove innocence or guilt is through a credible witness. The testimony of that witness will either corroborate or disprove the defendant's claim of innocence. So, if we humans try to adhere to some form of justice in our society, then how much greater will God's justice be? (Psalm 89.14) God would not even let Israel condemn a man to die unless it was corroborated by two or more witnesses; one was insufficient to pass such a judgment. (Numbers 35.30, Deuteronomy 17.6) The Calvinist teaching of predestination is tantamount to God passing judgment on those whose guilt is corroborated by zero witnesses, which is utterly preposterous.

61

There is none more righteous, upright, holy, just, merciful, or loving than God. There have been, are, and will be those who do not believe the gospel of Jesus Christ. However, it will not be because they did not have a chance to accept it first. I realize this broaches on the topic of those who have never heard the gospel, which could easily be a book unto itself. Suffice it to say for now though, that all things will be brought under Christ according to God's purpose. Paul writes about this very thing in Romans 2.11-16 when dealing with contentions amongst the Jewish believers that Gentiles could not be saved because they didn't have, or know, the law. The quandary of which is settled by him in verse 16 when he says, "In the day when God shall judge the secrets of men by Jesus Christ according to my gospel." To that I can only add, amen.

Matthew 28.19-20 Go ye therefore, and teach all nations, baptizing them in the name of the Father, and of the Son, and of the Holy Ghost: Teaching them to observe all things whatsoever I have commanded you: and, lo, I am with you alway, even unto the end of the world. Amen. (KJV)

The last earthly command given by Jesus to His disciples was what is known as The Great Commission, which are the two verses above. His directive was not for the disciples to seek out the predestined, or the chosen. It was for them to go to all nations. Once again, we see that Christ is sending His gospel into all the world. The very premise of teaching is to impart knowledge that was heretofore unknown on the part of the one being taught. It would have been completely illogical for the Savior to direct His disciples to go and teach His gospel to those His Father had previously declared lost. However, it would be entirely logical to direct them to teach those whom had never heard His gospel, knowing as He did, that Holy Spirit was coming behind Him to convict the world of sin. (John 16.8)

Mark 14.9 Verily I say unto you, Wheresoever this gospel shall be preached throughout the whole world, this also that she hath done shall be spoken of for a memorial of her. (KJV)

Not about predestination, just another general statement from the Savior that indicates who He came to save. Here He was making mention of the act of Martha, sister of Lazarus, who had anointed

His feet with expensive oil. Which, upon seeing, the disciples, Judas Iscariot in particular, noted that the oil could have been sold and the proceeds given to the poor. Jesus tells them that what Martha has done will be remembered wherever the 'gospel shall be preached throughout the whole world'. Maybe this seems an insignificant factor where the topic of predestination is concerned, but still is *prima facie* evidence that the Savior fully intended for His gospel to be perpetuated all over the world.

This verse typifies what I mean by examining the whole of Scripture, as it might otherwise seem that it has no relation to anything we have been discussing. However, the Word of God is knit together so well that there are no ravels, no runs, no pulls, and no holes within it. Everything, even the motives of the Savior, are on display in everything He says and does. The Word reveals His heart in every matter of the gospel, and there can be nothing within Scripture that would contradict Him. Anything that appears contradictory in the Word is due to man's misunderstanding of the Spirit's inspiration of its writers. Remember, one of Holy Spirit's original tasks upon His arrival was to instruct the writers of what would become the New Testament (John 16.13-14).

Mark 16.15 And he said unto them, Go ye into all the world, and preach the gospel to every creature. (KJV)

Here we have Mark's version of the Great Commission. In it Jesus gives the same command we see in Matthew's gospel, which is very explicit, "Go ye into all the world". How much more direct could the Savior be? He has been with the disciples a little over three years teaching them and preparing them for this moment. This is the greatest undertaking in human history, Christ has come to save the world and someone has to go and tell them about it. Yet, Jesus did not instruct the disciples to seek out the chosen, the elect, or the predestined. He did not reveal to them the ones they were looking for had already been chosen by His Father before time began.

If the doctrine of predestination as taught by Calvinism were in fact true, then it would be the prevailing thought in all of these seemingly unrelated Scriptures. Yet, it is not. The only motive, attitude, or direction that is seen in the Bible concerning the perpetuation of the gospel is that it be global, always. When Christ talks, he talks about taking the gospel to the world. When the disciples write, they write about Jesus being the Savior of the world. There are absolutely no Scriptures that even hint that the gospel is for none less than the entirety of humankind. Look at what John says about Jesus in his great discourse at the beginning of his gospel:

John 1.9 That was the true Light, which lighteth every man that cometh into the world. (KJV)

That 'true Light' is of course Jesus Christ, and any thing, or any one that claims to be the true Light, save Jesus Christ, is false. Jesus called His followers the 'light of the world' in an earlier passage, but that is because the light that we shine is a reflection of the true Light, it is not our own. John says of the true Light that He lights every man (human) in the world. That is saying the gospel of Jesus shall be made known to all mankind regardless of when they lived upon this earth. His gospel shines the light of His witness to all, so that there shall be no one that can say that they have not heard it. True, that when many have the light of the gospel shine upon them they turn from it and run back to their darkness. However, the light has been shown upon them, and it is they who have chosen to go back to darkness.

John 3.17 For God sent not his Son into the world to condemn the world; but that the world through him might be saved. (KJV)

The verse after John 3.16 is just as good as it is. Once again, this is Christ discussing with Nicodemus what it means to be saved. In three direct statements to Nicodemus, Christ makes reference that He has come for the salvation of the world, or for all mankind. Notice, as well, in this verse that Jesus explains one of His functions in the plan of salvation, that He did not come to 'condemn', but to 'save'. There will come a time for judgment, but this is not that time. Now is the time that He has come to secure redemption for fallen mankind, as was determined from before the foundation of the world.

If God had indeed declared who was saved, and who was lost before the foundation of the world this would have been tantamount to condemnation. Yet, Christ tells us that the Father has not sent Him to condemn, and so why would He do this if He knew that there were those who were already condemned. The reason why He could do this is because His Father never made such a decree about the salvation of any man before the foundation of the world. You see, the Bible tells us in Hebrews 9.27, "And as it is appointed unto men once to die, but after this the judgment." (KJV) And by this we know that our judgment (condemnation) is reserved until after our death, for appointment by its very nature denotes a future event.

Christ Himself says the very same thing. The time for condemnation was not yet, for Jesus says in plain and direct language why the Father had sent Him, "...that the world through him might be saved." Not that the 'elect' might be saved, not that the 'chosen' might be saved, and not that the 'predestined' might be saved, but 'the world'. I am reminded here of Paul's admonition to young Timothy to hold fast to "...the simplicity that is in Christ." (2 Corinthians 11.3)

THE SIMPLICITY OF CHRIST

Allow me to expand a little upon the thought I ended the last chapter with, that being, as Paul said, "...the simplicity of Christ." I have read numerous Calvinist writings that want to admonish people for doing just that, to make the Word of God too simple. This is not to engage in debate with those who hold these beliefs, for those who would debate the issue are likely the same ones who are not going to relent of their beliefs regardless of what anyone says or writes. However, this attitude must be addressed for those who are still in 'search mode' regarding certain theological issues that remain unsettled in their life. In fact, I think I would be pretty safe in making the statement, as broad as it may be, that there are probably about 'zero' people on this planet right now who have it all figured out...just going out on a limb there.

Let me take a moment to reiterate something that I touched on earlier, which was regardless of who you are, where you are, and what kind of shape your life is in, God loves you. If you remember nothing else you read in this work, remember that! This is not fluff to take up space on a page either; this is an admonition to you, the reader, that you are as important to the God of all creation as any other person in this world. Why in the world should God's Word not be simple? He is not trying to hide anything from anybody; in fact, just the opposite is true for He wants the entire world to know of His love for them. What can be so hard to understand about that? The only ones making things complicated are men.

Now, understand me though, I am not saying that anybody can sit down with the Bible and come away knowing the secrets of all existence. Nobody can do that because that is not what the Bible was given to us for, it is God's rescue beacon announcing the coming of our rescuer, Jesus Christ. It tells us exactly what we need to know to be saved, why we need to be saved, and how to live a pleasing life before our Creator, period. The Bible is not the window to God's soul, and as I told you earlier, there is not a person alive able to speak on His behalf concerning matters of His heart. But, many of those Calvinist writings I alluded to earlier cast doubt on whether anyone who believes that way even understands the sovereignty of God. I assure you, those of us who do not see predestination the way of the Calvinist are just as aware of God's sovereignty as any Calvinist. They do not have the market cornered on that, and neither do I.

There are things that you and I will never know on this side of eternity, regardless of what we call ourselves. So, when I refer to the simplicity of God's Word, I am speaking of that for which it was given which is namely, the salvation of mankind. John himself said at the end of his gospel that if all the things that Jesus did were recorded that the world probably couldn't contain the books, and that was from three and a half years of ministry. What in the world do you think the books would look like if the deeds of the Godhead from eternity past were all recorded? It would be just like God, beyond our human comprehension. The Bible serves a specific purpose for mankind, the exact purpose that God intends it to serve, the salvation of the world.

Yes, there are going to be things you don't understand, but then again, that's all of us. So, you see the inherent danger of the Calvinist teaching of predestination, which is that someone who thinks their lack of understanding of the deep things of God translates into them not being among the predestined. This in itself could lead to many unfortunate circumstances, such as anger at God, resentment that they were not chosen, depression, and withdrawal from the church, but they all end with a sinner being denied the love of their Creator. Not because they were shunned by God, but because they were misled by men. This is completely unacceptable from someone claiming the moniker of Christian.

Consider this, remember the claim that I have made several times in this work that God never decreed from the foundations of the world who was saved and who was lost? Well, that statement is a deduction. That being, I cannot give you proof in your hands that will prove that claim beyond all doubt. How could I, for I was not present then, obviously? However, neither were you, or anybody else that has ever walked on this earth, save One. So, while I cannot unequivocally prove He didn't, neither can the Calvinist prove He did. That Scripture does not exist.

However, what I do have is what I am giving you now, a whole Book full of statements telling me that God sent His Son into this world to save whosoever will believe in Him. Hence, I have 'deduced' by the fact that God sent His Son to save us, that He has yet to condemn us to eternal lostness. So, although I do not have that concrete proof, the circumstantial evidence is overwhelming. If this were a matter of something that did not affect people's salvation (the teaching of predestination according to Calvinism), then it would simply be another hotly debated theological topic. However, it does affect people's salvation, and thus must be dealt with. This is not the rapture, where some believe this and some believe that, but the result is irrelevant to ones salvation. This is a life or death battle that has the potential to send people to a hell that was not meant for them, so the Christian has no other alternative than to confront it.

The only way to confront it though is with the truth, or the Truth of the Word to be more precise. It is incomprehensible to me how one can take a word (predestine) that appears only a handful of times (depending on your translation) and suddenly be an expert on what God was doing before we were even created (they may say I'm doing the same thing, but I'll get to that). God did not give us the Bible to chronicle His doings before we were around. He gave it to point us to Jesus. It is always about Jesus, always has been, always is, and always will be. All in the world that this nonsense (the teaching of the predestination of man) has done for the last two thousand years is take the focus off of Jesus. When Augustine was teaching it, when Calvin was teaching it, when Spurgeon was teaching it, and when the reformers of today teach it, it draws attention away from where it should be, on Jesus Christ.

So then, how can I be so confident that I know what God was doing before we were created when I have just admonished the Calvinist for doing the same thing. I have only one claim, that being the whole of Scripture. That is all in this world that I base my claim on, for I have nothing else. I can only tell you what I believe when I look at the overall theme of Scripture, that God sent His Son to save any who will believe in Him. Time and time and time again, the Bible speaks about the Savior coming to save the world. It is woven all throughout the Bible, unlike the four or five verses that have a form of the word predestine in them. These verses have been made to cast derision on God's Word by the Calvinist, and that is a shame. These verses are part of the whole of Scripture, not some hidden doctrine tucked away in God's Word for the theological elite.

All that I know about the happenings before the foundation of the world are what are told in Scripture, and those are covered in this work. And, these reveal that it is Jesus Christ that is the lamb slain before the foundation of the world. It was Jesus Christ that was chosen by His Father to execute salvation's plan. It was Jesus Christ elected and predestined to fulfill the requirements for mankind's redemption. It was Jesus Christ that was foreknown of His Father that all those that were yet to be created could claim these same things through Him (Jesus), and through Him only. Thus, I am compelled by the logic endowed me by my Creator to come to the conclusion that God has not yet decreed who is saved and who is lost, for Holy Spirit is still about His work of drawing all who will believe to Jesus.

Whatever your conclusion in this matter might be, only know one thing...make up your own mind. Do not let me, the Calvinist, the preacher, the pope, the priest, any denomination, any author, any singer, any TV evangelist, or anybody else tell you what God has planned for your life. None of us know what God has in store for you, and if we tell you we do we're lying. The very notion that the created can counsel on behalf of the Creator belittles the very gospel that was sent to save us. Your relationship with God is an extremely personal matter to Him, so much so that He sent His Son to settle it, and Holy Spirit to negotiate it. This is a matter that you must decide for yourself. All in the world that any of us can ever do is to point others to the one who saved us, and leave the rest up to Holy Spirit.

John 6.33 For the bread of God is he which cometh down from heaven, and giveth life unto the world. (KJV)

The sixth chapter of John gives the account of Jesus feeding the multitudes (five thousand men, plus their families), after which Jesus walked on the water later that night when the disciples were crossing the sea (Lake Galilee). In the verse above, the multitudes, or some of them at least, have made their way across to where Jesus is at, and are now asking Him for further proof that He is indeed the One to come (the Messiah). Jesus is explaining to them that although they think that the miracle of the children of Israel in the wilderness being fed with manna was the 'bread from heaven', that it is indeed He who is the bread from heaven (i.e., Bread of God). He also adds that, unlike the manna that was for Israel, He has come to give "life unto the world".

After this announcement, the crowd then asks Him to give them this bread, to which He makes the proclamation once again that He is the bread of life. Then after this He makes a statement that reformed theology has used to indicate that the predestination of man is factual:

John 6.37-39 All that the Father giveth me shall come to me; and him that cometh to me I will in no wise cast out. For I came down from heaven, not to do mine own will, but the will of him that sent me. And this is the Father's will which hath sent me, that of all which he hath given me I should lose nothing, but should raise it up again at the last day. (KJV)

Jesus twice makes a statement about those that the Father 'gives' Him, which to the Calvinist means those God has predestined. These verses exemplify splendidly the danger of taking verses, or passages, out the context of the whole of Scripture. If you stop at verse 39 you will misconstrue the intent of the Saviors message. Because, notice that Jesus speaks also about doing the will of the One who sent Him (God). And, in the succeeding verse, explains precisely what God's will is concerning Him (Jesus):

John 6.40 And this is the will of him that sent me, that every one which seeth the Son, and believeth on him, may have everlasting life: and I will raise him up at the last day. (KJV)

So, as revealed by the Son, the will of the Father is that anyone who sees the Son, and believes on Him may have eternal life. Thus, we know that God's will is for every one who sees and believes, or at least we should. To demonstrate what I am getting at, imagine that you have never read a word of the Bible, and that you know absolutely nothing of Jesus Christ, or His gospel. If you pick up the Bible and read this one verse above, how do you think you will interpret it? Knowing nothing of Christ you would interpret it exactly as anyone would, you would think that you needed to actually see the Son, and then believe on Him to have eternal life. That is what it says, so naturally you would think that.

My point is this, the Bible is a whole, and it must be understood as such. We do not have the prerogative to pick and choose what we want to out of it and make doctrine of some passages, while discounting others. Yes, this is hyperbole, but the point remains, we can never remove individual passages from within the context of the whole of Scripture. We know from Scripture that what Christ is speaking of is 'seeing' with faith, and not 'seeing' with the eyes. We also know that when Christ says that His grace and mercy are available to every one, then that means every one for that too is corroborated by the whole of Scripture. Just because He uses the phrase 'all that the Father gives me' does not mean the message of the gospel has changed. That phrase, and any like it (i.e., the elect, the chosen, etc.) simply denotes a subset of those that the Father desires to see saved, namely 'every one'. It does not mean those are the only ones to whom salvation is intended as He reiterates further on in the chapter:

John 6.51 I am the living bread which came down from heaven: if any man eat of this bread, he shall live for ever: and the bread that I will give is my flesh, which I will give for the life of the world. (KJV)

Jesus is still talking to the crowd, and He is telling them that as the physical body must have 'bread' (food/nourishment) to sustain it, so too must our spirit be sustained if it is to live. However, this spiritual nourishment that Jesus is speaking of must come at the expense of His physical person (…bread…is my flesh), and those in attendance are having a hard time comprehending what He means. But, even still, He tells them that His flesh is given for "…the life of the world", although very few at the moment understand it significance. In fact, what He says is so troubling that by the end of this chapter, many of those who are called His disciples will leave from following

Him, with only the twelve remaining (John 6.60 & 66). The very idea of their Messiah coming as a servant, much less as a sacrifice for the sins of the world, was not what the Jewish people were expecting.

The Messiah was supposed to come in majesty and glory. He was to throw off the yoke of pagan bondage placed upon Israel by their Roman oppressors. He was to be the King of Israel, the King of the Jews. Yet, this man (Jesus) that some have believed could actually be the One foretold that would come, is now telling them He must die to give them life. And, even beyond that, He is talking about giving life, not just to Israel, but also to the entire world. To the Gentiles of all people! These are the people the Messiah was supposed to liberate them (Israel) from, not join them to. When the discourse is finished, and all is said and done, Jesus stands alone with the twelve disciples He had chosen. Yes, those He had chosen, for we have seen that any choosing, electing, or predestining come exclusively in, and through, Jesus Christ. Only now, He is doing it live and in person. Christ had extended the invitation for the twelve to follow, and they had accepted that call.

Much is made by reformed theology about the fact that Jesus makes this, and several statements like this, throughout the gospels about 'choosing' these. However, it is quite evident from Scripture just exactly what Jesus is referring to when He speaks of choosing His disciples. This being, that they have been chosen as the ones 'entrusted' with seeing that His gospel be spread to 'all the world' after He is gone. These few years in time were, are, and will always be the single most important time in all of human history. They shall stand for all eternity. They are recorded in Heaven and Earth, and shall always be remembered and celebrated. I believe Jesus had very specific reasons to choose the twelve He did. He says as much in one of those passages that Calvinism likes to fall back on, His famous prayer just before His crucifixion:

John 17.6 I have manifested thy name unto the men which thou gavest me out of the world: thine they were, and thou gavest them me; and they have kept thy word. (KJV)

This is at the beginning of the prayer of Jesus, which encompasses the entire seventeenth chapter of John. In this request of His Father,

Jesus acknowledges that He has completed the task given to Him, "…manifested thy name…", and that these the Father 'gave' Him have 'kept thy word'. Then He further adds:

John 17.9 I pray for them: I pray not for the world, but for them which thou hast given me; for they are thine. (KJV)

Jesus prays specifically for the disciples, "…for them…not for the world", which He says have been given to Him from the Father. These passages are used by Calvinist to support their assertion that God has chosen some for salvation, while condemning others to lostness, and if these were the only two verses in Scripture then they might have a point. But, they are not, for they are a short statement, within a larger prayer, within a larger life that must be a taken in the context of the larger whole of Scripture. For even within this very same prayer, in fact, in the next verse Christ prays these words:

John 17.20 Neither pray I for these alone, but for them also which shall believe on me through their word. (KJV)

So, Jesus prays first for the disciples (verse 19), and then prays for "…them also which shall believe on me…" (verse 20), which in itself is an open ended request not restricted by any qualifier, except that they 'believe'. Yet, notice how these come to believe, "…through their (the disciples) word". This is that moment in history that I spoke of earlier, this is the greatest event that will ever happen. The news (gospel) concerning the redemption of all mankind is about to be proclaimed, and Christ has handpicked those whom He wants to represent Him on the world's stage. This prayer is not a treatise on the doctrine of predestination, it is a prayer. A prayer of a thankful servant that is grateful for His Heavenly Father's blessings.

The Father 'gave' Jesus these (the disciples) just as He (God) gives any of us anything. The air we breathe, the food on our tables, our family, our friends, our health, everything good in our lives all comes from God. What in the world is so hard to understand about that? We are not actors and actresses playing out our part in some grand divine production where our every word, deed, thought, or action is all scripted out for us. Neither, are we a race of programmed individuals with no capacity of thought and reason, and unable to decide what we will do or not do. No, we are the creation of a Loving, Compassionate, albeit, Just Creator who desires to have a relationship with us. Jesus further explains in the next two verses:

John 17.21-22 That they all may be one; as thou, Father, are in me, and I in thee, that they also may be one in us: that the world may believe that thou hast sent me. And the glory which thou gavest me I have given them; that they may be one, even as we are one: (KJV)

This is not the prayer of a Savior who was sent to save the predestined few, this is the prayer of the Savior of the world, all the world. Why would it even matter if the predestined were one (in unity) or not? They have already been chosen haven't they? Why would Jesus care if the world believed the Father sent Him or not? What does that have to do with anything if the predestined are already saved, and the condemned are already lost? It is entirely irrational, and illogical to think that Jesus Christ has nothing less than the entirety of all of mankind in mind when He prays this prayer.

There is an inherit sadness that must strike us, as Christians, in the above prayer of Christ, "…that they may also be one in us: that the world may believe that thou hast sent me." How many people have rejected the gospel of Christ because of the way those who say they follow Him act? Our (Christian) unity determines the effectiveness of our Savior's gospel, as Christ Himself has said. Yet, we become embroiled in bickering and infighting over this or that doctrine, and all the while the world looks on in amusement that those who claim to serve the Creator of all that exists can't even get along themselves. Only, there is nothing even remotely amusing about it. Our disunity profanes the Kingdom of God, and our Savior's gospel.

We far too often confuse the Righteous, Sovereign King of the Universe with that humble, lowly servant that stepped into time two thousand years ago to secure our redemption. If indeed we claim His redemption of our souls, then we must also claim His Lordship over every aspect of our lives. We are truly "…not our own", for the price He paid for us entitles Him to rule our life (1 Corinthians 6.19-20). The time has far passed that those who claim the blood of Christ put aside all matters such as fighting over whose doctrine is correct or not, and place all of our focus and attention where it is due, on Jesus Christ. This is what our King wants for us:

John 17.23 I in them, and thou in me, that they may be made perfect in one; and that the world may know that thou hast sent me, and hast loved them, as thou hast loved me. (KJV)

"Perfect in One", how much could we accomplish for the Kingdom of God if we could but realize this in our lives. Not only does Christ want the world to know that the Father sent Him for their rescue, but He wants them to know how much He (God) has loved them. Jesus says that He (God) has loved the world, as He loves Jesus. Let that sink in, for this is life altering and you will never be the same. This is the message that we need to be proclaiming to the lost world, not I'm right and he's wrong. Only when we are able to accept God's unconditional love shown to us through His Son, and revealed to us by Holy Spirit, will we be able to understand the importance of this as it pertains to His Kingdom. May God help us to show His Love.

IN THE BEGINNING

In this concluding chapter I want to talk about what I consider the most overwhelming evidence that Jesus Christ came to save any and all who would only believe in Him. I sincerely believe that in the light of this evidence there is no logical explanation for someone to believe in the individual predestination of man. However, before I present this evidence I want to say a word about where it comes from. Certainly, it comes from the Bible, but it is where in the Bible it comes from that I believe holds such significance, namely, the book of Genesis.

While the Bible in general is looked upon with disdain by the world we live in, it is quite safe to say that there has never been a more scrutinized and vilified work than the book of Genesis. There are even countless numbers of those within church walls each week who are content to relegate the accounts in Genesis to myth and folklore. While I shall delve into this matter in great detail in the forthcoming book *Creation: The Biblical Truth Series*, I do feel it necessary to touch on the subject in this work. I have mentioned several times within this work that we do not have the prerogative to simply pick and choose what we will accept out of God's Word, and what we will discount. If possible, this is even truer with the first eleven chapters of Genesis.

It is in these chapters that the foundation of Scripture rests. These chapters explain the majesty and sovereignty of our Creator, as much as is in our ability to understand, and why we are indeed a one of a kind creation that is so very special to Him. It is these chapters that reveal why Jesus had to come in the first place, and even foretell His coming. The seeds of all faith are found within their pages. For how could someone not understand that the One that created all that exists out of nothing is more than capable of saving us from our sordid state. The One who created in six days is the One who holds time in His hands. Yes, six twenty-four hour days.

All of the theistic evolution, day-age theory, gap-theory, or any other compromise of God's Word is absurd. The only thing literal about any of them is that they are literal nonsense. God's Word is the standard by which all others are measured, not the other way around. Men do not decide what God meant with His words, God speaks, and it is thus. This is why I feel so adamant that even the question of predestination is unequivocally answered within the first few chapters of Genesis. Let us look at what happened there:

Genesis 3.6-7 And when the woman saw that the tree was good for food, and that it was pleasant to the eyes, and a tree to be desired to make one wise, she took of the fruit thereof, and did eat, and gave also unto her husband with her; and he did eat. And the eyes of them both were opened, and they knew that they were naked; and they sewed fig leaves together, and made themselves aprons. (KJV)

The passage above describes the account of what happened when Eve, being deceived by Satan, disobeyed God. While there might be those who would lay this sin at the feet of Eve, that is simply not the case. Notice, that Eve immediately gives the fruit to Adam after she eats of it. Thus, Adam is right there with her the entire time these events are transpiring. To understand the significance of this let us look back a chapter:

Genesis 2.16-18 And the LORD God commanded the man, saying, Of every tree of the garden thou mayest freely eat: But of the tree of the knowledge of good and evil, thou shalt not eat of it: for in the day that thou eatest thereof thou shalt surely die. And the LORD God said, It is not good that the man should be alone; I will make him an help meet for him. (KJV)

There was but one command to be followed in the garden, and it was given to Adam personally by God, and it was given to him before God created Eve. Thus, it was Adam's responsibility to make sure the command was followed. We know that he (Adam) had told Eve by the time of the deception because she too tells Satan that God has commanded them not to eat of that tree. Therefore, Eve is aware of the command that they not eat of the tree by way of being told so by

Adam. However, God has personally charged Adam with the keeping of the command, and thus the responsibility rest solely with him, and as he was present he should have rebuked Satan with God's Word.

The fact that Adam alone was responsible for disobeying God is evidenced in His pronouncement of judgment upon them. For Eve, God proclaimed that pain in childbirth would be multiplied, and that her desire would now be to her husband. But, He did not lay the sin to her charge, for there was no pronouncement of death (Romans 6.23). However, notice God's judgment upon Adam:

Genesis 3.17-19 And unto Adam he said, Because thou hast hearkened unto the voice of thy wife, and hast eaten of the tree, of which I commanded thee, saying, Thou shalt not eat of it: cursed is the ground for thy sake; in sorrow shalt thou eat of it all the days of thy life; Thorns also and thistles shall it bring forth to thee; and thou shalt eat the herb of the field; In the sweat of thy face shalt thou eat bread, till thou return unto the ground; for out of it wast thou taken: for dust thou art, and unto dust shalt thou return. (KJV)

Adam got the death sentence. Notice that because of his sin, God pronounced, "...cursed is the ground for thy sake", for sin had entered into what God had said was "very good" (Genesis 1.31). Thus, because of Adam's sin, all of creation was now cursed with death. The decay had begun.

Therefore, through the sin of one man, Adam, all of his progeny (mankind) would now be born into a world of sin. The curse brought death to, not only mankind, but also to everything that God had created and placed under his stewardship. We are born into a world in which we are already separated from God, because He does not abide where there is sin. Where once the Son of God came down and fellowshipped with Adam and Eve (Genesis 3.8), now that fellowship had been broken. It remains broken for everyone born into this world still today. It is the work of Jesus Christ that made it possible for that relationship to be restored upon the conviction of ones sin by Holy Spirit.

And what does this have to do with the teaching of the predestination of mankind? Remember that the Calvinist version of predestination teaches that God chose individuals for salvation, and others for condemnation before the world began. Such a decree by God would have effectively negated the very act of disobedience by Adam in the garden. I realize the Calvinist will vehemently disagree with this conclusion; however, they cannot have it both ways. By that I mean that their staunch adherence to God's sovereignty allows them to say that He knew who would believe, and who would not. Thus, by His decree of the predestined before time began the matter would have been settled, and yet they also say that Christ still had to come and pay the price for the sins of those who would believe, and that Holy Spirit still had to come and convict those who would be saved of their sins. It simply cannot be both ways.

However, if God is as sovereign as the Calvinist claim, which by the way I wholeheartedly believe that He is, then His decree before time began would have settled the matter. It cannot be both ways if God's sovereignty is absolute, which it most certainly is. Therefore, as God is absolutely sovereign, then one of two things must be true, either 1) God never made the decree of who was saved and who was lost, or 2) Jesus Christ came to earth in vain. This is the quandary that the predestination camp has been trying to explain for almost two thousand years.

It is utterly preposterous to even think that it would be possible for God to send His Son when He didn't have too, much less to believe it. Now, I would be remiss if I did not make absolutely clear here that I do not think there are any Calvinist whatsoever that believe that either. However, I do think that they have become so entrenched in a culture of circular reasoning that they have blindly overlooked what is such a glaring contradiction within their theology. So, while I know that there are none that actually believe that, their logic belies their beliefs.

So, how does Adam fit into all this? The apostle Paul does an excellent job of explaining that:

Romans 5.12-15 Wherefore, as by one man sin entered into the world, and death by sin; and so death passed upon all men, for that all have sinned: (For until the law sin was in

the world: but sin is not imputed when there is no law. Nevertheless death reigned from Adam to Moses, even over them that had not sinned after the similitude of Adam's transgression, who is the figure of him that was to come. But not as the offence, so also is the free gift. For if through the offence of one many be dead, much more the grace of God, and the gift by grace, which is by one man, Jesus Christ, hath abounded unto many. (KJV)

If you were not overly familiar with the 5th chapter of Romans, now would be a good time to go back and review it. This is definitely some good reading. Here in the passage above, Paul begins to explain the universal implications of Adam's sin and says that, "…death passed upon all men" because of the actions (sin) of one man (Adam). Paul also says that Adam is a type of Christ, in that the actions of the one affect all, when he says, "…who is the figure of him that was to come", which was of course, Jesus Christ. However, while Adams posterity received the curse of death, the posterity of Christ would receive the 'free gift' of life.

I have read the literature, the books, and the articles from the Reformers who all point to this, and others verses like this, which they say conclusively proves that Christ came to save "many" and not all. However, one needs only to read the entire passage above to understand that to make that conclusion, one would have to take what Paul is saying completely out of context. Yes, he does use the word 'many' when referring to Christ, but so too does he use 'many' when referring to the reach of Adam's offense right before that. And, we know from verse 14 that Paul implicitly understands that the reach of that offense was "…all men".

Even further, notice that Paul says that though this offense has affected all men, "…much more the grace of God, and the gift by grace…" shall Christ's actions abound to mankind. Paul is clear that as Adam's sin is universal in its effects, so much more is the grace of God, through Jesus Christ, universal in its reach. It is complete and utter negligence to focus in on Paul's use of the word 'many', and try to argue that he meant 'not all'. When the context of the entire passage clearly dictates that he meant 'all'. If there should be any doubt, look at what Paul says only three verses later, still in the context of what he is speaking about:

Romans 5.18 Therefore as by the offence of one judgment came upon all men to condemnation; even so by the righteousness of one the free gift came upon all men unto justification of life. (KJV)

This passage seals the deal on the Calvinist teaching of predestination. When one reads the entirety of Romans 5, it is clear what Paul is saying. Remember, it was Paul who wrote to Timothy about the "...simplicity that is in Christ". Paul is, in my humble estimation, a straight shooter, he does not mince words, and he most certainly says what he means. I believe he writes in a no-nonsense manner in which all his readers need do to understand what he is saying is to simply employ common sense. Such is the case here in his letter to the church at Rome. He is not expounding some mysterious hidden doctrine, nor is he trying to write a letter that had to be deciphered in order to be understood.

He tells the church plainly that Adam's sin has brought death to all, and he tells them just as plainly that Christ's gift has brought life to all. Christ is the beginning and the end of redemption's work, there is nothing left save for a person to choose whether they believe Christ did this for them, or not. It is that simple. Just as God allowed Adam to choose what he would do in the garden, so too does He allow us to choose what we will do with Christ. Will we choose death, or choose Life?

If you went back and read all of Romans 5 then you saw these verses:

Romans 5.6-8 For when we were yet without strength, in due time Christ died for the ungodly. For scarcely for a righteous man will one die: yet peradventure for a good man some would even dare to die. But God commendeth his love toward us, in that, while we were yet sinners, Christ died for us. (KJV)

Notice who it was that Paul tells us Christ died for, "...the ungodly", and ask yourself who do you think that is? Can there really be any debate about that anyway? Paul does not say, "Christ died for the elect", nor "Christ died for the chosen", nor does he say, "Christ died for those His Father foreknew", and he doesn't say, "Christ died for the predestined". No, he says, "Christ died for the ungodly". That was I before He saved me, that was you before He saved you, and that is everybody that has ever been conceived since time began. We are, or were at one time, all ungodly.

And yet, Paul says Christ died for us. He adds that barely would any of us think of giving our life for someone 'righteous', and maybe, just maybe, for someone 'good', but for some ungodly sinner, no way. But how great is God's Love! So great that He sent His Son for me, that ungodly sinner that wasn't worth saving. So great that He sent His Son for you. And yes, oh thank God yes, He sent His Son for all mankind, that if any who choose to believe in Him then they too can be saved. Blessed be the name of the Father, Son, and Holy Spirit.

Romans 11.33 O the depth of the riches both of the wisdom and knowledge of God! how unsearchable are his judgments, and his ways past finding out! (KJV)

Amen.

BIBLICAL REFERENCES

This section includes references to passages within Scripture in the book where the corresponding verses are not listed in their entirety.

Introduction

Hebrews 10.19-22 Having therefore, brethren, boldness to enter into the holiest by the blood of Jesus, By a new and living way, which he hath consecrated for us, through the veil, that is to say, his flesh; And having an high priest over the house of God; Let us draw near with a true heart in full assurance of faith, having our hearts sprinkled from an evil conscience, and our bodies washed with pure water. (KJV)

Malachi 3.6 For I am the LORD, I change not; therefore ye sons of Jacob are not consumed. (KJV)

2 Peter 3.9 The Lord is not slack concerning his promise, as some men count slackness; but is longsuffering to us-ward, not willing that any should perish, but that all should come to repentance. (KJV)

The Love of God

Ecclesiastes 3.11 He hath made every thing beautiful in his time: also he hath set the world in their heart, so that no man can find out the work that God maketh from the beginning to the end. (KJV)

Isaiah 55.11 So shall my word be that goeth forth out of my mouth: it shall not return unto me void, but it shall accomplish that which I please, and it shall prosper in the thing whereto I sent it. (KJV)

1 Timothy 2.5 For there is one God, and one mediator between God and men, the man Christ Jesus. (KJV)

John 1.1-3 In the beginning was the Word, and the Word was with God, and the Word was God. The same was in the beginning with God. All things were made by him; and without him was not any thing made that was made. (KJV)

Revelation 4.11 Thou art worthy, O Lord, to receive glory and honour and power: for thou hast created all things, and for thy pleasure they are and were created. (KJV)

1 Peter 1.18-21 Forasmuch as ye know that ye were not redeemed with corruptible things, as silver and gold, from your vain conversation received by tradition from your fathers; But with the precious blood of Christ, as of a lamb without blemish and without spot: Who verily was foreordained before the foundation of the world, but was manifest in these last times for you, Who by him do believe in God, that raised him up from the dead, and gave him glory; that your faith and hope might be in God. (KJV)

John 16.8-11 And when he is come, he will reprove the world of sin, and of righteousness, and of judgment: Of sin, because they believe not on me; Of righteousness, because I go to my Father, and ye see me no more; Of judgment, because the prince of this world is judged.

John 3.16 For God so loved the world, that He gave His only begotten Son, that whosoever believeth in Him should not perish, but have everlasting life. (KJV)

Malachi 3.6 For I am the LORD, I change not; therefore ye sons of Jacob are not consumed. (KJV)

James 1.17 Every good gift and every perfect gift is from above, and cometh down from the Father of lights, with whom is no variableness, neither shadow of turning. (KJV)

Psalm 102.27 But thou art the same, and thy years shall have no end. (KJV)

John 12.31-32 Now is the judgment of this world: now shall the prince of this world be cast out. And I, if I be lifted up from the earth, will draw all men unto me. (KJV)

Matthew 28.18-20 And Jesus came and spake unto them, saying, All power is given unto me in heaven and in earth. Go ye therefore, and teach all nations, baptizing them in the name of the Father, and of the Son, and of the Holy Ghost: Teaching them to observe all things whatsoever I have commanded you: and, lo, I am with you alway, even unto the end of the world. Amen. (KJV)

Joel 2.32 And it shall come to pass, that whosoever shall call on the name of the LORD shall be delivered: for in mount Zion and in Jerusalem shall be deliverance, as the LORD hath said, and in the remnant whom the LORD shall call. (KJV)

Matthew 5.19 Whosoever therefore shall break one of these least commandments, and shall teach men so, he shall be called the least in the kingdom of heaven: but whosoever shall do and teach them, the same shall be called great in the kingdom of heaven. (KJV)

Matthew 7.24 Therefore whosoever heareth these sayings of mine, and doeth them, I will liken him unto a wise man, which built his house upon a rock. (KJV)

Matthew 10.14 And whosoever shall not receive you, nor hear your words, when ye depart out of that house or city, shake off the dust of your feet. (KJV)

Matthew 10.32-33 Whosoever therefore shall confess me before men, him will I confess also before my Father which is in heaven. But whosoever shall deny me before men, him will I also deny before my Father which is in heaven. (KJV)

Matthew 12.50 For whosoever shall do the will of my Father which is in heaven, the same is my brother, and sister, and mother. (KJV)

Matthew 16.25 For whosever will save his life shall lose it: and whosoever will lose his life for my sake shall find it. (KJV)

Matthew 18.4 Whosever therefore shall humble himself as this little child, the same is greatest in the kingdom of heaven. (KJV)

Mark 3.35 For whosoever shall do the will of God, the same is my brother, and my sister, and mother. (KJV)

Mark 8.34-35 And when he had called the people unto him with his disciples also, he said unto them, Whosoever will come after me, let him deny himself, and take up his cross, and follow me. For whosoever will save his life shall lose it; but whosoever shall lose his life for my sake and the gospel's, the same shall save it. (KJV)

Luke 6.47 Whosoever cometh to me, and heareth my sayings, and doeth them I will shew you to whom he is like. (KJV)

Luke 7.23 And blessed is he, whosoever shall not be offended in me. (KJV)

Luke 9.24 For whosever will save his life shall lose it: but whosoever will lose his life for my sake, the same shall save it. (KJV)

Luke 9.26 For whosoever shall be ashamed of me and of my words, of him shall the Son of man be ashamed, when he shall come in his own glory, and in his Father's, and of the holy angels. (KJV)

Luke 9.48 And said unto them, Whosoever shall receive this child in my name receiveth me: and whosoever shall receive me receiveth him that sent me: for he that is least among you all, the same shall be great. (KJV)

Luke 12.8 And I say unto you, Whosoever shall confess me before men, him shall the Son of man also confess before the angels of God. (KJV)

Luke 14.27 And whosoever doth not bear his cross, and come after me, cannot be my disciple. (KJV)

Luke 17.33 Whosoever shall seek to save his life shall lose it; and whosoever shall lose his life shall preserve it. (KJV)

Luke 18.17 Verily I say unto you, Whosoever shall not receive the kingdom of God as a little child shall in no wise enter therein. (KJV)

John 3.15-16 That whosoever believeth in him should not perish, but have eternal life. For God so loved the world, that he gave his only begotten Son, that whosoever believeth in him should not perish, but have everlasting life. (KJV)

John 4.13-14 Jesus answered and said unto her, Whosoever drinketh of this water shall thirst again: But whosoever drinketh of the water that I shall give him shall never thirst; but the water that I shall give him shall be in him a well of water springing up into everlasting life. (KJV)

John 11.26 And whosoever liveth and believeth in me shall never die. Believest thou this? (KJV)

John 12.46 I am come a light into the word, that whosoever believeth on me should not abide in darkness. (KJV)

Acts 2.21 And it shall come to pass, that whosoever shall call on the name of the Lord shall be saved. (KJV)

Acts 10.43 To him give all the prophets witness, that through his name whosoever believeth in him shall receive remission of sins. (KJV)

Acts 13.26 Men and brethren, children of the stock of Abraham, and whosoever among you feareth God, to you is the word of this salvation sent. (KJV)

Romans 9.33 As it is written, Behold, I lay in Zion a stumblingstone and rock of offence: and whosoever believeth on him shall not be ashamed. (KJV)

Romans 10.11 For the scripture saith, Whosoever believeth on him shall not be ashamed. (KJV)

Romans 10.13 For whosoever shall call upon the name of the Lord shall be saved. (KJV)

Galatians 5.4 Christ is become of no effect unto you, whosoever of you are justified by the law; ye are fallen from grace. (KJV)

James 2.10 For whosoever shall keep the whole law, and yet offend in one point, he is guilty of all. (KJV)

1 John 2.23 Whosoever denieth the Son, the same hath not the Father: but he that acknowledgeth the Son hath the Father also.(KJV)

1 John 3.6 Whosoever abideth in him sinneth not: whosoever sinneth hath not seen him, neither known him. (KJV)

1 John 3.9-10 Whosoever is born of God doth not commit sin; for his seed remaineth in him: and he cannot sin, because he is born of God. In this the children of God are manifest, and the children of the devil: whosoever doeth not righteousness is not of God, neither he that loveth not his brother. (KJV)

1 John 4.15 Whosoever shall confess that Jesus is the Son of God, God dwelleth in him, and he in God. (KJV)

1 John 5.18 We know that whosoever is born of God sinneth not; but he that is begotten of God keepeth himself, and that wicked one toucheth him not. (KJV)

Revelation 20.15 And whosoever was not found written in the book of life was cast into the lake of fire. (KJV)

Revelation 22.17 And the Spirit and the bride say, Come, And let him that heareth say, Come. And let him that is athirst come, And whosoever will, let him take the water of life freely. (KJV)

"End of the whosoever's"

Matthew 27.51 And, behold, the veil of the temple was rent in twain from the top to the bottom; and the earth did quake, and the rocks rent. (KJV)

Mark 15.38 And the veil of the temple was rent in twain from the top to the bottom. (KJV)

Luke 23.45 And the sun was darkened, and the veil of the temple was rent in the midst. (KJV)

Hebrews 9.11-14 But Christ being come an high priest of good things to come, by a greater and more perfect tabernacle, not made with hands, that is to say, not of this building; Neither by the blood of goats and calves, but by his own blood he entered in once into the holy place, having obtained eternal redemption for us. For if the blood of bulls and goats, and the ashes of an heifer sprinkling the unclean, sanctifieth to the purifying of the flesh: How much more shall the blood of Christ, who through the eternal Spirit offered himself without spot to God, purge your conscience from dead works to serve the living God? (KJV)

Hebrews 10.19-25 Having therefore, brethren, boldness to enter into the holiest by the blood of Jesus, By a new and living way, which he hath consecrated for us, through the veil, that is to say, his flesh; And having an high priest over the house of God; Let us draw near with a true heart in full assurance of faith, having our hearts sprinkled from an evil conscience, and our bodies washed with pure water. Let us hold fast the profession of our faith without wavering; (for he is faithful that promised;) And let us consider one another to provoke unto love and to good works: Not forsaking the assembling of ourselves together, as the manner of some is; but exhorting one another: and so much the more, as ye see the day approaching. (KJV)

John 16.7-14 Nevertheless I tell you the truth; It is expedient for you that I go away: for if I go not away, the Comforter will not come unto you; but if I depart, I will send him unto you. And when he is come, he will reprove the world of sin, and of righteousness, and of judgment: Of sin, because they believe not on me; Of righteousness, because I go to my Father, and ye see me no more; Of judgment, because the prince of this world is judged. I have yet many things to say unto you, but ye cannot bear them now. Howbeit when he, the Spirit of truth, is come, he will guide you into all truth: for he shall not speak of himself; but whatsoever he shall hear, that shall he speak: and he will shew you things to come. He shall glorify me: for he shall receive of mine, and shall shew it unto you. (KJV)

1 Timothy 2.5 For there is one God, and one mediator between God and men, the man Christ Jesus. (KJV)

Luke 24.13-49 And, behold, two of them went that same day to a village called Emmaus, which was from Jerusalem about threescore furlongs. And they talked together of all these things which had happened. And it came to pass, that, while they communed together and reasoned, Jesus himself drew near, and went with them. But their eyes were holden that they should not know him. And he said unto them, What manner of communications are these that ye have one to another, as ye walk, and are sad? And the one of them, whose name was Cleopas, answering said unto him, Art thou only a stranger in Jerusalem, and hast not known the things which are come to pass there in these days? And he said unto them, What things? And they said unto him, Concerning Jesus of Nazareth, which was a prophet mighty in deed and word before God and all the people: And how the chief priests and our rulers delivered him to be condemned to death, and have crucified him. But we trusted that it had been he which should have redeemed Israel: and beside all this, to day is the third day since these things were done. Yea, and certain women also of our company made us astonished, which were early at the sepulchre; And when they found not his body, they came, saying, that they had also seen a vision of angels, which said that he was alive. And certain of them which were with us went to the sepulchre, and found it even so as the women had said: but him they saw not. Then he said unto them, O fools, and slow of heart to believe all that the prophets have spoken: Ought not Christ to have suffered these things, and to enter into his glory? And beginning at Moses and all the prophets, he expounded unto them in all the scriptures the things concerning himself. And they drew nigh unto the village, whither they went: and he made as though he would have gone further. But they constrained him, saying, Abide with us: for it is toward evening, and the day is far spent. And he went in to tarry with them. And it came to pass, as he sat at meat with them, he took bread, and blessed it, and brake, and gave to them. And their eyes were opened, and they knew him; and he vanished out of their sight. And they said one to another, Did not our heart burn within us, while he talked with us by the way, and while he opened to us the scriptures? And they rose up the same hour, and returned to Jerusalem, and found the eleven gathered together, and them that were with them, Saying, The Lord is risen indeed, and hath appeared to Simon. And they told what things were done in the way, and how he was known of them in breaking of bread. And as they thus spake, Jesus himself stood in the midst of them, and saith unto them, Peace be unto you. But they were terrified and affrighted, and supposed that they had seen a spirit. And he said unto them, Why are ye troubled? and why do thoughts arise in your hearts? Behold my hands and my feet, that it is I myself: handle me, and see; for a spirit hath not flesh and bones, as ye see me have. And when he had thus spoken, he shewed them his hands and his feet. And while they yet believed not for joy, and wondered, he said unto them, Have ye here any meat? And they gave him a piece of a broiled fish, and of an honeycomb. And he took it, and did eat before them. And he said unto them, These are the words which I spake unto you, while I was yet with you, that all things must be fulfilled, which were written in the law of Moses, and in the prophets, and in the psalms, concerning me. Then opened he their understanding, that they might understand the scriptures, And said unto them, Thus it is written, and thus it behoved Christ to suffer, and to rise from the dead the third day: And that repentance and remission of sins should be preached in his name among all nations, beginning at Jerusalem. And ye are witnesses of these things. And, behold, I send the promise of my Father upon you: but tarry ye in the city of Jerusalem, until ye be endued with power from on high. (KJV)

John 17.1-5 These words spake Jesus, and lifted up his eyes to heaven, and said, Father, the hour is come; glorify thy Son, that thy Son also may glorify thee: As thou hast given him power over all flesh, that he should give eternal life to as many as thou hast given him. And this is life eternal, that they might know thee the only true God, and Jesus Christ, whom thou hast sent. I have glorified thee on the earth: I have finished the work which thou gavest me to do. And now, O Father, glorify thou me with thine own self with the glory which I had with thee before the world was. (KJV)

John 12.23-32 And Jesus answered them, saying, The hour is come, that the Son of man should be glorified. Verily, verily, I say unto you, Except a corn of wheat fall into the ground and die, it abideth alone: but if it die, it bringeth forth much fruit. He that loveth his life shall lose it; and he that hateth his life in this world shall keep it unto life eternal. If any man serve me, let him follow me; and where I am, there shall also my servant be: if any man serve me, him will my Father honour. Now is my soul troubled; and what shall I say? Father, save me from this hour: but for this cause came I unto this hour. Father, glorify thy name. Then came there a voice from heaven, saying, I have both glorified it, and will glorify it again. The people therefore, that stood by, and heard it, said that it thundered: others said, An angel spake to him. Jesus answered and said, This voice came not because of me, but for your sakes. Now is the judgment of this world: now shall the prince of this world be cast out. And I, if I be lifted up from the earth, will draw all men unto me. (KJV)

John 1.1 In the beginning was the Word, and the Word was with God, and Word was God. (KJV)

The Real Predestination

John 15.18 If the world hate you, ye know that it hated me before it hated you. (KJV)

1 Corinthians 1.27-31 But God hath chosen the foolish things of the world to confound the wise; and God hath chosen the weak things of the world to confound the things which are mighty; And base things of the world, and things which are despised, hath God chosen, yea, and things which are not, to bring to nought things that are: That no flesh should glory in his presence. But of him are ye in Christ Jesus, who of God is made unto us wisdom, and righteousness, and sanctification, and redemption: That, according as it is written, He that glorieth, let him glory in the Lord. (KJV)

Psalm 89.2 For I have said, Mercy shall be built up for ever: thy faithfulness shalt thou establish in the very heavens. (KJV)

Hebrews 3.16-19 For some, when they had heard, did provoke: howbeit not all that came out of Egypt by Moses. But with whom was he grieved forty years? was it not with them that had sinned, whose carcases fell in the wilderness? And to whom sware he that they should not enter into his rest, but to them that believed not? So we see that they could not enter in because of unbelief. (KJV)

2 Peter 3.9 The Lord is not slack concerning his promise, as some men count slackness; but is longsuffering to us-ward, not willing that any should perish, but that all should come to repentance. (KJV)

Matthew 28.19-20 Go ye therefore, and teach all nations, baptizing them in the name of the Father, and of the Son, and of the Holy Ghost: Teaching them to observe all things whatsoever I have commanded you: and, lo, I am with you alway, even unto the end of the world. Amen. (KJV)

Romans 8.28-29 And we know that all things work together for good to them that love God, to them who are the called according to his purpose. For whom he did foreknow, he also did predestinate to be conformed to the image of his Son, that he might be the firstborn among many brethren. (KJV)

2 Timothy 1.9 Who hath saved us, and called us with an holy calling, not according to our works, but according to his own purpose and grace, which was given us in Christ Jesus before the world began. (KJV)

Romans 1.16 For I am not ashamed of the gospel of Christ: for it is the power of God unto salvation to every one that believeth; to the Jew first, and also to the Greek. (KJV)

2 Timothy 2.10 Therefore I endure all things for the elect's sakes, that they may also obtain the salvation which is in Christ Jesus with eternal glory.

Romans 16.25-27 Now to him that is of power to stablish you according to my gospel, and the preaching of Jesus Christ, according to the revelation of the mystery, which was kept secret since the world began, But now is made manifest, and by the scriptures of the prophets, according to the commandment of the everlasting God, made known to all nations for the obedience of faith: To God only wise, be glory through Jesus Christ for ever. Amen.(KJV)

John 14.26 But the Comforter, which is the Holy Ghost, whom the Father will send in my name, he shall teach you all things, and bring all things to your remembrance, whatsoever I have said unto you. (KJV)

For The World

John 3.1 There was a man of the Pharisees, named Nicodemus, a ruler of the Jews. (KJV)

Numbers 21.4-9 And they journeyed from mount Hor by the way of the Red sea, to compass the land of Edom: and the soul of the people was much discouraged because of the way. And the people spake against God, and against Moses, Wherefore have ye brought us up out of Egypt to die in the wilderness? for there is no bread, neither is there any water; and our soul loatheth this light bread. And the LORD sent fiery serpents among the people, and they bit the people; and much people of Israel died. Therefore the people came to Moses, and said, We have sinned, for we have spoken against the LORD, and against thee; pray unto the LORD, that he take away the serpents from us. And Moses prayed for the people. And the LORD said unto Moses, Make thee a fiery serpent, and set it upon a pole: and it shall come to pass, that every one that is bitten, when he looketh upon it, shall live. And Moses made a serpent of brass, and put it upon a pole, and it came to pass, that if a serpent had bitten any man, when he beheld the serpent of brass, he lived. (KJV)

Revelation 13.8 And all that dwell upon the earth shall worship him, whose names are not written in the book of life of the Lamb slain from the foundation of the world. (KJV)

Genesis 2.7 And the LORD God formed man of the dust of the ground, and breathed into his nostrils the breath of life; and man became a living soul. (KJV)

Ezekiel 33.11 Say unto them, As I live, saith the Lord GOD, I have no pleasure in the death of the wicked; but that the wicked turn from his way and live: turn ye, turn ye from your evil ways; for why will ye die, O house of Israel? (KJV)

Psalm 89.14 Justice and judgment are the habitation of thy throne: mercy and truth shall go before thy face. (KJV)

Numbers 35.30 Whoso killeth any person, the murderer shall be put to death by the mouth of witnesses: but one witness shall not testify against any person to cause him to die. (KJV)

Deuteronomy 17.6 At the mouth of two witnesses, or three witnesses, shall he that is worthy of death be put to death; but at the mouth of one witness he shall not be put to death. (KJV)

Romans 2.11-16 For there is no respect of persons with God. For as many as have sinned without law shall also perish without law: and as many as have sinned in the law shall be judged by the law; (For not the hearers of the law are just before God, but the doers of the law shall be justified. For when the Gentiles, which have not the law, do by nature the things contained in the law, these, having not the law, are a law unto themselves: Which shew the work of the law written in their hearts, their conscience also bearing witness, and their thoughts the mean while accusing or else excusing one another;) In the day when God shall judge the secrets of men by Jesus Christ according to my gospel. (KJV)

John 16.8 And when he is come, he will reprove the world of sin, and of righteousness, and of judgment. (KJV)

John 16.13-14 Howbeit when he, the Spirit of truth, is come, he will guide you into all truth: for he shall not speak of himself; but whatsoever he shall hear, that shall he speak: and he will shew you things to come. He shall glorify me: for he shall receive of mine, and shall shew it unto you. (KJV)

2 Corinthians 11.3 But I fear, lest by any means, as the serpent beguiled Eve through his subtilty, so your minds should be corrupted from the simplicity that is in Christ. (KJV)

The Simplicity of Christ

John 6.60 Many therefore of his disciples, when they had heard this, said, This is an hard saying; who can hear it? ...

verse 66 From that time many of his disciples went back, and walked no more with him. (KJV)

1 Corinthians 6.19-20 What? know ye not that your body is the temple of the Holy Ghost which is in you, which ye have of God, and ye are not your own? For ye are bought with a price: therefore glorify God in your body, and in your spirit, which are God's. (KJV)

In The Beginning

Romans 6.23 For the wages of sin is death; but the gift of God is eternal life through Jesus Christ our Lord. (KJV)

Genesis 1.31 And God saw every thing that he had made, and, behold, it was very good. And the evening and the morning were the sixth day. (KJV)

Genesis 3.8 And they heard the voice of the LORD God walking in the garden in the cool of the day: and Adam and his wife hid themselves from the presence of the LORD God amongst the trees of the garden. (KJV)

ACKNOWLEDEMENTS

I wanted to take this opportunity to personally thank each of you who purchased and read this book. It is an honor and a privilege to be able to do something on behalf our Lord, especially where it involves those that He loves so dearly, the human race. It is my earnest prayer that those of us who know Jesus Christ as Lord and Savior of our lives will work in unity and love to continue the work of the Kingdom through the fulfillment of the Great Commission. May we ever carry the precious gospel to those who need to hear its message.

If you have read this work in order to gain a greater understanding of our Great God, it is also my prayer that you have been successful in that endeavor. Perhaps you are in search of something greater in your life, and I encourage you to continue in that quest. Our God is faithful in that He has promised that if we would earnestly seek Him, then He shall reward that search. Holy Spirit is ever present, and when He comes to invite you to believe in the Savior of all mankind, Jesus Christ, then you will have the opportunity to make the single greatest decision in your life. Keep searching.

The proceeds of this work go toward the work of the Kingdom through the endeavors of *davidsonministries*. I invite you to learn more about what we are doing through visiting our website at www.davidsonministries.org. What we do would not be possible without you, and for that you have our eternal gratitude. May God bless you!

J.Davidson

Mt 6.33

AUTHOR'S BIO

Joseph Davidson has been actively involved in Christian ministry as a minister of the gospel for the last 25 years. He has been married to his wife, Sonja, for the last 24 years, and they have been blessed with two daughters, Rebekah and Makenna. Joseph has recently founded *davidsonministries* as an avenue to take the gospel into areas which might not otherwise be reached. He also serves as the Student Pastor to a vibrant church in his home state of Georgia. Davidson's primary interests are his family, his church, and his ministry. He also enjoys reading a range of topics that are somewhat eclectic, as evidenced by his educational background. He holds a B.A. in Geology, an M.P.A., and a Masters of Divinity. He enjoys the study of science, history, and of course the Bible. Davidson is currently at work on the next book in *The Biblical Truth Series* that will focus on the creation account as told in Genesis. He anticipates an early 2014 release for that work. Find out more at www.davidsonministries.org.